D0342410

"The story of the Trocmés has given me much courage. Their example and story is for such a time as now."
—**Vickie Reddy**, founder of We Welcome Refugees and executive producer of The Justice Conference

"As the world confronts one of the greatest refugee crises in recorded history, this powerful true story could not be more timely or relevant."
—**Matthew Soerens**, coauthor of *Seeking Refuge* and U.S. director of church mobilization for World Relief

"A beautiful narrative of redemption and mercy in the midst of occupied France under the Nazi regime."
—**Mae Elise Cannon**, author of *Social Justice Handbook* and *Just Spirituality*

"*Love in a Time of Hate* quickens our holy imagination to see what is possible in this day at this time. . . . A gift to the church."
—**Margot Starbuck**, coauthor of *Overplayed* and author of *Small Things with Great Love*

"This story's main takeaway is timeless. Moral, nonviolent resistance is needed now more than ever before. Relevant at home and in the halls of power, this book calls on all modern-day Magdas to answer the door and act."
—**Michael Shank**, head of communications for the UN Sustainable Development Solutions Network

"A poignant message in our day and for our world: love must live and thrive in us in response to fear, division, and hatred."
—**Donald Peters**, executive director of Mennonite Central Committee Canada

LOVE
in a Time of
HATE

**The Story of Magda and André Trocmé
and the Village That Said No
to the Nazis**

LOVE
in a Time of
HATE

The Story of Magda and André Trocmé
and the Village That Said No
to the Nazis

Hanna Schott

Translated by John D. Roth

 **Herald Press**
Harrisonburg, Virginia

Library of Congress Cataloging-in-Publication Data
Names: Schott, Hanna, 1959- author.
Title: Love in a time of hate : the story of Magda and André Trocmé and the
    village that said no to the Nazis / Hanna Schott.
Other titles: Von Liebe und Widerstand. English
Description: English edition. | Harrisonburg, Virginia : Herald Press, 2017.
Identifiers: LCCN 2016054730| ISBN 9781513801254 (pbk. : alk. paper) |
    ISBN 9781513801599 (ebook)
Subjects: LCSH: Trocmé, André, 1901-1971. | Trocmé, Magda, 1901-1996. |
    Righteous Gentiles in the Holocaust—France—Le
    Chambon-sur-Lignon—Biography. | Pacifists—France—Le
    Chambon-sur-Lignon—Biography. | Holocaust, Jewish (1939-1945) —France—Le
    Chambon-sur-Lignon. | World War, 1939-1945—Jews—Rescue—France—Le
    Chambon-sur-Lignon. | World War, 1939-1945—Underground
    movements—France—Le Chambon-sur-Lignon. | Le Chambon-sur-Lignon
    (France) —History—20th century.
Classification: LCC D804.66.T76 S3613 2017 | DDC 940.53/18092244595—
dc23 LC record available at https://lccn.loc.gov/2016054730

Love in a Time of Hate is based on *Von Liebe und Widerstand: Magda und André Trocmé*, first published in German in 2012 by Neufeld Verlag, VdK-Strasse, 92521 Schwarzenfeld, Germany. This English edition is published by agreement with Neufeld Verlag. Translated from the German by John D. Roth.

Unless otherwise noted, Scripture text is quoted, with permission, from the *New Revised Standard Version*, © 1989, Division of Christian Education of the National Council of Churches of Christ in the United States of America.

Scripture quotations marked (NIV) are taken from the Holy Bible, New International Version®, NIV®. Copyright © 1973, 1978, 1984, 2011 by Biblica, Inc.™ Used by permission of Zondervan. All rights reserved worldwide. www.zondervan.com The "NIV" and "New International Version" are trademarks registered in the United States Patent and Trademark Office by Biblica, Inc.™

Contents

Foreword

It was like any other Thursday morning. As I scrolled through Instagram in the summer of 2015, I was confronted with the image of the dead body of three-year-old Alan Kurdi, washed up on a beach in Turkey. I sat and stared at the photograph. I realized that a country—multiple countries, in fact—were being devastated as we sat blindly by. As *I* sat blindly by.

I wondered what it was going to take to get me to pay attention. And what I was willing to do about it.

A year and a half earlier, I had stood in Yad Vashem, the World Holocaust Remembrance Center in Jerusalem, wondering how the world sat by and watched the extermination of millions of Jews during the Holocaust. I have considered other genocides and atrocities from recent history and wondered the same thing. How did the world sit by and allow this to happen? How did ordinary citizens like you and me sit by quietly and not speak out?

And suddenly, looking at that image of little Alan Kurdi's body, I realized: We've been here before. The atrocities taking place now are not new. And our response, or lack thereof, is not new. We are allowing history to repeat itself. We are still choosing to look away, rather than responding actively with love, embracing, welcoming, and providing for those who desperately need it.

As I have endeavored to speak out for refugees, the vulnerable, and the oppressed, I constantly return to the Word of God. Jesus says in Matthew 25:

> "I was hungry and you fed me,
> I was thirsty and you gave me a drink,
> I was homeless and you gave me a room,
> I was shivering and you gave me clothes,
> I was sick and you stopped to visit,
> I was in prison, and you came to me."

Then those "sheep" are going to say, "Master, what are you talking about? When did we ever see you hungry and feed you, thirsty and give you a drink? And when did we ever see you sick or in prison and come to you?" Then the King will say, "I'm telling the solemn truth: Whenever you did one of these things to someone overlooked or ignored, that was me—you did it to me." (Matthew 25:35-40 *The Message*)

As I read this passage, I am not sure how much clearer Jesus needed to be. He didn't say, "Feed and protect and visit only when it is convenient, or when you are not at risk, or when you have all the answers, or when the government leads the way." He says, simply, that when we do these things, we are doing them to him.

I keep asking: Where is the church right now? Where are the followers of Jesus? What are we doing in response to the greatest humanitarian crisis of our time?

When I came across this book, *Love in a Time of Hate*, my heart was stirred, my resolve strengthened. We have been here before. And there were those who chose love over fear, those who chose to run headfirst into uncertainty and to respond as Jesus commanded.

André and Magda Trocmé's story is so, so very important. Their story—of choosing to love their neighbors in a time when hate was so prevalent—challenges us to not allow fear or complicity with injustice to be our response.

The lessons in this story are so timely for what we are facing in the world and the church today. Can we learn from history? Can we learn from those who have gone before?

André and Magda allowed their lives to be completely interrupted and their path to be completely orchestrated by God. They submitted to God's authority at each step, regardless of the personal cost. They were willing to follow God rather than conform to what went against their conscience. As followers of Jesus, they saw the image of God in every person, and they refused to stand silent in the face of wrong.

The Trocmés lived at a time when the ways of peace were cast to the side; yet they fought for these values, committed to teaching them to others and living them out themselves. They could not have known just how tested these values would become. I wonder this for myself. As I choose the way of peace and welcoming and loving my neighbor, what will God require of me? And how will I answer?

The story of the Trocmés has given me much courage. Their example and story is for such a time as now. May we listen and learn.

—Vickie Reddy,
founder of We Welcome Refugees
and executive producer of The JUSTICE Conference

Prologue

I t was a cold winter evening. Magda Trocmé stoked the fire in the oven in her kitchen. Through the kitchen window she saw that fresh snow had fallen. Her husband, a minister, was traveling. The children were already asleep in bed. Suddenly, the doorbell rang.

Outside, weakly illuminated by the light that extended from the doorway into the street, stood a woman. She was dressed much too lightly for the weather and was trembling from the cold. The sandals she wore on her bare feet sank into the snow.

"Come in!" said Magda. She noted by the woman's response— "Merci, Madame"—that the woman spoke with a German accent. The woman was a Jew. She had been wandering somewhat aimlessly in France for several weeks, searching for a haven from the Nazis and their French collaborators. Someone had told her about the village of Le Chambon, and that there was a pastor there to whom one could turn for help.

"Sit down," Magda said. "Are you hungry?"

***

13

"Whoever does not love God will always be dividing humans into races, classes, or other kinds of groups," Magda's husband, André, had preached in a sermon years before that snowy evening. "We, on the other hand, know that God abides in the soul of every human being. Every human can find God there, can hear God's voice. Every human possesses the capacity to look within, where God can always be revealed. Sometimes this even happens without us being aware of it. God's love for humans teaches us how we too are to love. . . . Every human is a bearer of God's image in the world."

The snow, the fire in the hearth, the children in bed, the doorbell: these sound like the things of legend. The events that made Magda and André Trocmé famous have indeed become things of legend, and André's words about God's love are now, through the lens of history, prophetic. That evening in the kitchen, in which a conspiracy of love began, contained the elements of a fairytale.

But these are the simple facts: one cold winter evening during World War II, the doorbell at the front entrance of the parsonage rang.

And Magda opened the door.

PART I

1

Motherless World

Florence and Rome, 1901–9

The king of Italy made an imposing sight. Little Magda stood before his oil portrait in wonder. Whoever wore so many stars, bands, buttons, medals, and baubles, in addition to a sash, was without a doubt the most important and powerful man in all of Italy. And right after him came Papa.

The similarity in moustaches and medals made it clear that the two men were good friends. The king had a funny-looking beard—its tips turned upward so that they pointed at his ears. Papa's moustache was shorter, and his ears did not stick out from under his hat the way the king's did. Clearly, Papa was the better looking of the two, even though he had fewer medals on his chest.

"Papa rode past our house with his soldiers": In one of her very first childhood memories, Magda stood on the balcony and watched the parade pass in front of their house. Papa was seated on a majestic horse. The army band marched in front of him. Papa was a colonel. Magda had no idea what that meant, but the word sounded like *colonna*: column. Papa was as slender and handsome as a column. He was so important that he was not able to live at home. Papa stood watch over the entire land.

Oscar Grilli di Cortona could have claimed that he did in fact belong to the columns that upheld the Italian monarchy. At the time of the parade that Magda remembered, her father was stationed at the *fortezza* of Florence, close to where the family's house was located.

A large, dark figure standing at the end of a long, dark hallway and calling Magda to run into his arms: that was Magda's second childhood memory. The man was wearing a black coat that reached to the floor, and a tall black hat was perched on his head. She was afraid and had no interest in doing what he requested. Magda did not know that the black-clad figure was a monk who belonged to the Russian Orthodox Church, whose worship services took place several floors below the Grilli family's apartment in Rome, not far from the Vatican. She felt nothing other than fear.

Florence, Rome: Oscar Grilli di Cortona was stationed for several years in both places, but "Rome" or "Florence" meant nothing to a three- or four-year-old child. The only things she knew in either place were rooms with high ceilings, unimaginably long, badly lit hallways, dark red carpets, and an old-style, doorless elevator that moved slowly in a loop up and down inside the building without stopping.

There was little difference in the ambiance of the two places Magda lived—only the governesses changed, in a yearly rhythm. The "older sisters" who arrived from the north—the phrase *au pair* had not yet been invented—made their Italian sojourn and traced Goethe's steps in Florence, Naples, and Rome. And there, where they settled for a few months, they took care of a rather terrified little girl and tried to teach her the things they considered the most important.

***

Magda's parents, Nelly Wissotzky and Oscar Grilli di Cortona.
Private collection.

Magda grew up in a motherless world. Nelly Wissotzky Grilli di Cortona, Magda's mother, died at the age of twenty-three, ten months after her marriage and barely four weeks after the birth of her daughter.

Magda's world was a motherless world, but it was nevertheless a world full of women.

There was Varia Wissotzky Poggio, whom Magda called Grand-Maman. She was Magda's maternal grandmother, and probably the person in the Grilli household best suited to provide little Magda with something like maternal care and to establish an emotional bond with the child. Grand-Maman spoke French with her granddaughter, and they addressed each other in the formal style. Sometimes, however, they shifted to English or German, and when Magda was not supposed to understand the conversation, the adults present slipped into Russian. Grand-Maman had been born in Siberia.

How did a child from Florence come to have a Siberian grandmother? The story was complicated but quite typical for a time in which the concept of an "immigrant background" had not yet been invented. People searching for a better life were on the move in every corner of Europe.

Grand-Maman's father, Alexej Poggio, lived in Saint Petersburg. That he bore an Italian family name was because his father, a noble merchant from Genoa, had killed an opponent in a duel and was forced to flee from Italy to Russia. The dishonorable emigration of his father proved to be no obstacle to the young Alexej, who rapidly ascended in Russian society. Alexej first fought against Napoleon and then became a bodyguard in the czar's court. Until December 1825, he enjoyed a life of ease and glamor in the royal household. Then a new czar, Nicholas I, succeeded his father on the throne. In a solemn ceremony, the officers of the guard were supposed to swear an oath before their new lord. But they refused to do so. In their view, the Russian crown was standing in the way of long-overdue reforms. Serfdom, especially, should have been eliminated long ago—and for that conviction the officers were ready to risk life and limb. Alexej was fortunate that he was not numbered among the leaders of the rebellion; they were immediately hanged. The other rebels, who later became known as Decembrists, were demoted and banished to Siberia. Alexej was part of this group, and he remained there for thirty years until Alexander II ascended the throne and commuted the punishment of the Decembrists.

Thus it came to be that Grand-Maman was born in Siberia. A life that began in Siberia and led to Tuscany gave Grand-Maman the ability to adapt and made her curious about every new thing she encountered.

Regardless of the day or season, Grand-Maman always wore black. And, at least in the judgment of the fashion-conscious Italian relatives, she was always poorly dressed. "Someday someone on the street is going to come up to you and slip you some coins," said Nonna Grilli, Magda's paternal grandmother, who was always alert to the visible markers that distinguished her family from the common folk.

"Then I'll take the money and give it to someone who can use it," Grand-Maman answered decisively.

Grand-Maman had been trained in Geneva and Florence as a pianist, but she also nurtured a deep love of philosophy and literature. When Magda was a bit older, her grandmother held animated conversations with her about the Russian side of her family history, the question of serfdom, and the struggle of the Decembrists. Magda surely would have heard the term *human rights* for the first time from the mouth of Grand-Maman. But then there were also all the routine matters, as well as Italian. Grand-Maman quizzed Magda when it came time for exams;

sometimes she was learning the content alongside her grand-daughter. Grand-Maman was clearly the favorite grandmother—perhaps even an older friend—and now and then in later years an accomplice as well. But she was never tender with Magda. Taking the child on her lap and giving her a kiss would have been, for Grand-Maman, unthinkable.

Grand-Maman never spoke of her daughter Nelly—Magda's deceased mother—and did not tolerate others speaking of her either. Both Nelly's life and Nelly's death were taboo subjects in the Grilli family. In Oscar Grilli's bedroom hung a photo of his deceased wife. It showed Nelly as a young, seemingly fragile, beautiful woman—the beloved, who remained such for Oscar's entire life.

"Do you know who that is?" Father once asked Magda. It was one of those rare days in which she visited him in his room.

"The woman in the photo?" Magda asked. "No. I don't know."

Was it that she couldn't say it—that the word *mama* could not pass her lips? Or did she truly not know? Years later, even the sixty-year-old Magda, when pressed by her children to speak into a tape recorder about her memories, could not answer this question.

***

A grand-papa belonged to Grand-Maman. He was not dead, but he was invisible. Grand-Maman never spoke of him, but every now and then a small gift would arrive in the mail for Magda, sent by Grand-Papa from some mysterious place. Where this was, however, and why her grandfather never allowed himself to be seen like other grandfathers were some of the many mysteries of Magda's childhood.

The second woman in Magda's early world was Nonna Grilli, her father's mother. Mannered, strict, and status-conscious, she was a native Italian, but she only conversed in French. For her, Italian served only to give instructions to servants and delivery boys. Between Nonna Grilli and Magda stood first the wet nurses and then a comet's tail of governesses, in keeping with all the standard conventions of the family's class.

The third woman who also lived in the house and helped to shape Magda's life and perspective was Aunt Olga, Nelly's sister and Magda's aunt. But she too was as good as invisible, even though she slept only a few steps away in a darkened, adjoining bedroom. Day after day she lay there on her chaise longue. Aunt Olga suffered from migraines, and for several years it was Magda's dream to share in her suffering. Whoever had migraines got tea from the servants and the best pastries, which you could receive in bed along with a great deal of care and attention. Whoever had migraines didn't have to repeat her piano lessons endlessly or practice perfect handwriting. She could simply be there and do nothing at all. What a life!

Aunt Olga's daughter Lalli was the fourth female presence in Magda's world. These two cousins, nearly the same age, developed a profound trust for each other. Their friendship was the one glimmer of light in Magda's childhood.

Lalli's family was also without a man in the house. Her father had left the family shortly after Lalli's birth and had married another woman. Out of all of this, young Magda drew a clear conclusion: I have a father. Lalli has a mother. Some children must have a father, while others have a mother. Since people at that time were slow to correct the assumptions of children, Magda's conviction that she had no mother was not shaken for many years.

The fact that she too had once had a mother did not become clear through some child-appropriate explanation regarding conception and birth. Rather, she learned of her mother's existence in a coarse, almost brutal, manner. One day Magda overheard one of the household servants say to another: "È lei che ha ammazzato sua madre!" (She is the one who killed her mother). At first Magda didn't know whom they were talking about, but then she saw that the other maid was looking straight at her. They were talking about her! *She* had killed her mother?

The sentence pierced her heart. Magda could not free herself from the thought. And she knew not a single person in whom she could confide about such matters.

2

Magda's Fears

Florence, 1910–11

agda's father did not wear his heart on his sleeve. Perhaps expressing his feelings simply didn't fit with Oscar Grilli di Cortona's character and temperament. Or perhaps all young men in his circle placed their feelings behind shields so that they could become useful officers and worthy representatives of their social rank.

Only one stirring of his heart could not be hidden from those around him: Oscar's love for Elena Wissotzky Poggio, better known as Nelly. Magda's mother was the love of his life. She was certainly that in life, and she remained that in death as well. Nothing about this changed when Oscar remarried. For years he had resisted the expectations of his friends and counselors. A man, especially one in his position, must be married, they argued. Oscar would have gladly continued to live his life as he expected: successful in his career, yet lonely and withdrawn in private. But he finally relented. After nine years as a widower, he allowed himself to be persuaded to enter into a second marriage.

He chose Marguerite—a Florentine Italian Catholic. Oscar and Marguerite were married on December 1, 1910, and they absorbed Magda into their newly established home—at least on Sundays. For Marguerite, the nine-year-old stepchild was something like the leftover remains of her husband's past life. It was not that she did not like children. In time, Marguerite herself became the mother of three children, and she was not unhappy in this role. But Magda was the lingering memory of her husband's first marriage and—much more importantly—a reminder of her husband's great love.

That this love endured, and would continue to endure, soon became clear to Marguerite. Oscar carried a photo of Nelly in his wallet, wore her ring on his pinkie finger, and kept a lock of her hair in a chain around his neck. All this from a man who appeared to be anything but a romantic! Magda would later describe her father's marriage to Marguerite as a tragedy. Marguerite was driven sick with jealousy. Her feelings were directed not only at Nelly but also at Magda, even though Magda's father had never displayed any visible sign of attentiveness or tenderness to his daughter.

Marguerite's attitude never changed in the many years of their marriage, and her anxious possessiveness of her husband made Magda jealous in turn. But nothing could erase Oscar's deep connection to Nelly. Even as an old man he would read the letters his fiancée had written to him decades earlier. What's more, he copied them out in his own hand. Again and again he attempted to copy Nelly's signature so that at least the last word of these duplicated letters would appear as if written by her. After his death, all of these letters, along with the brooch containing the lock of Nelly's hair, were passed along to Magda.

***

Anyone living in the higher circles of Florentine society who was nearly eight years old was old enough to leave the house to pursue an education. So it was that Magda was sent to a boarding school run by German deaconesses, the Istituto delle Diaconesse di Via Santa Monica, on the other side of the Arno River. In 1860, the Kaiserswerther sisters, as they were called, had established a "house of education and nurture," in which they offered the children of Tuscany basic instruction comparable to a primary-school education today. It ended with an entrance exam into a state school, which for most students marked the end of their educational journeys.

When Magda was a student at the school in 1909, almost all the deaconesses were quite elderly; several of them had even known Magda's grandmother, Nonna Grilli, when she was a student there. Magda was the youngest of the female students, and her bed in the large dormitory was so high off the ground that she had to have a running start to jump into it. In the morning she had to make the bed with great care so that none of the blanket edges betrayed any hint of a wrinkle. Every Thursday evening the children were permitted to receive visitors, but only in the cool, dark "Hall of Emperors," whose portraits glowered sternly from the walls.

Grand-Maman appeared there dependably and punctually every Thursday, and brought Magda the local news and assured the unhappy, homesick child that they would see each other again on Sunday—that is, as long as Magda conducted herself beyond reproach. The school's standard punishment for a misdeed was that one could not go home for a Sunday visit.

Even Sunday began with the deaconesses. Grand-Maman came to the Sunday school at the boarding house to accompany the children's singing with the pump organ, but it would have been unthinkable to go directly from Sunday school to the noon

meal at Papa's house. First Grand-Maman and her granddaughter attended the so-called Swiss church, that is, the Waldensian
congregation,[1] where the two listened to a sermon in French
for nearly an hour—or, as was more often the case for Magda,
yearned for it to end. By then Magda would become restless, since
she knew that time was pressing and that she needed to be back
at the boarding school by suppertime. Indeed, as she later wrote,
soon after the meal with Papa and Marguerite, she would become
"overwhelmed with a feeling that my heart was constricting, my
hands began to feel cold and began to cramp. Soon I would need
to be heading back on the narrow Santa Monica alley!"

Once a week, as a charitable activity of the Salvation Army,
Grand-Maman distributed cod liver oil to the children in the
poor section of the neighboring San Frediano. How eagerly
Magda wished she were one of those poor children who were able
to be so close to Grand-Maman! Instead, she sat and thought
intently about her grandmother, only a few steps away, whom she
was not permitted to see.

The Istituto delle Diaconesse was a Protestant island in
Catholic Florence. Oscar had an English grandmother and therefore belonged to the Anglican Communion. Grand-Maman
was raised in the Russian Orthodox Church but had become a
Protestant in Italy and belonged to the Waldensians. The pastor
of the Waldensian congregation was also the one who had buried
Magda's mother and had asked, after Nelly's funeral, "Has the in-
fant been baptized?" Naturally, amid all the concern for the health
of the seriously ill mother, no one had given any thought to the
baptism of the child. So the pastor baptized Magda on the day of
the funeral, and with that act Magda also became a Protestant.

---

1 The Waldensian Church was founded by Peter Waldo in the twelfth
century. The Roman Catholic Church viewed Waldensians as heretics, and
in the sixteenth century, the Waldensians became part of the Protestant
Reformation. Waldensians became active in saving Jews during World War II.

***

Being different from the mainstream was one of the founda-tional, formative experiences of Magda's life. She was not like common people; she was aristocratic. She was not like all the other Catholics; she was Protestant. She was related not only to a Florentine family but to a Russian one as well. All of this fash-ioned her into a distinct individual, even as it also placed a heavy burden on her young shoulders. The life of an ordinary Florentine citizen was by no means uninteresting to her or something she dismissed. It was precisely because she knew so little about that world that it was full of mysterious and miraculous possibilities.

There was, for example, the prayer for the dead. "In the course of our time together with the deaconesses," Magda wrote years later, "Ada Gay [a fellow student who had lost both parents] and I had discovered that there was such a thing as prayer for the dead. Those who had died went either to hell or to paradise; however, most were in purgatory. This prayer could help them climb out of this unpleasant place to God. What happiness to discover this! Now we could help our mothers enter into heaven! We were not Catholic, but we recited a part of this prayer nonetheless in our own invented fantasy Latin."

Soon thereafter, Magda discovered that, according to her Catholic friends, all Protestants were destined for hell. Was her mother therefore not in purgatory, and would prayers of the daughter have no effect? Magda made some inquiries and dis-covered that those who had never in their earthly lives heard the Truth (with a capital *T*) would indeed be sent to purgatory and not directly to hell. Had her mother ever encountered the Truth? Magda preferred not to think very hard about it.

Alongside the comforting features of purgatory, the Catholics also had lots of holidays that were not granted to the Protestants. The deaconesses celebrated all of these in the full German style, and for the children the beloved Nikolas Day and Christmas festivals were the highlights of the year. On the other hand, August 15—the Assumption of the Virgin Mary—occurred in the middle of the summer holiday and in the full summer heat, and Magda had to study with Grand-Maman. Nonetheless, she especially enjoyed this day, even though she knew that for the Protestants it was Jesus who ascended into heaven; for the Catholics it was the Virgin Mary. "She seemed so attractive to me—this Virgin Mary!" Magda recalled.

> Holding a child in her arm, she looked at you and smiled. She was a mother. She was more interesting than Jesus. I didn't have a mother and didn't care for this man—Jesus on the cross with horrible wounds. In the Catholic church there were also lots of these bloody crucifixes all around; but to see this little Jesus in the arms of his mother was so good, so beautiful, so tender. With her small feet the Virgin mother trampled a snake made of red wax. The snake was horrifying, spewing fear and danger; but the mother of Jesus forced his head into the ground and stamped this evil creature to death. I loved that!

The Protestant churches were drab and strict, but the Catholic churches were beautiful, colorful, gilded, and filled with flickering candles. There were flowers that smelled so good and incense whose aroma permeated the entire church even when there was no worship service. "It was a mysterious odor that I had encountered nowhere else," Magda reflected. "Was that enough to become Catholic? The fear of hell and the beauty of the churches? Was that reason enough?"

In any case, Marguerite, Magda's Catholic stepmother, was very pleased with Magda's attraction to all things Catholic, and it was she who saw to Magda's transfer to a private Catholic school, the Istituto Frascani Signorini, after the completion of her studies with the deaconesses. And indeed, the desire grew in Magda to celebrate Communion with all the other children—to wear a white dress and to simply and truly belong. At home (if one could call the residence of her father a home), she felt less connected than ever. Marcella, her first half sister, had been born in the meantime, and the baby and wet nurse had taken over Magda's room. In her new bedroom—a small, dark space at the end of the hallway that led into the inner courtyard—Magda experienced still greater fears than those she had already known from the time she was a little child.

My fears grew and grew. At night I would lie for hours on my back with my eyes wide open so that I could keep a sharp watch on both the left and the right side of my bed. I wished so badly that my bed would at least have had one side against the wall; then I could have lain on my side and relaxed a little bit since I would need to guard only one side. But no. That was impossible because it made the cleaning difficult, or so they said. Furthermore, my fears were foolish.

I affixed two electric wires to my bed—one that led to a light and one that led to a bell so that one could use it to call the maid. In the dark I would worry: Were both wires still in place? I needed to look once more, and in the course of my search for them, the wires would fall to the ground so that I needed to find and connect them all over again.

When I was little I often told myself, "I am afraid, but now my governess is sleeping next to me; and later in life my husband will sleep next to me." But between my governess and my husband how many terrible, unsettled nights I had to endure!

In many of the worst nights, I got out of bed and crept, my back always to the wall, to the toilet. Along the way I had to look at a part of the wall to the right and the left and then the space above me. But what was there to see? Exactly that was the problem—this fear of everything and of nothing; the fear of the unexplainable.

Would a conversion to Catholicism eliminate these fears from her world? Magda hoped so. Grand-Maman, given all the conflicts that were already present in the family, preferred to say nothing about it. But Papa Oscar, when he considered the question carefully, regarded it as a good idea: a Catholic daughter would surely be easier to marry.

3

Finishing School

Florence, 1911–18

W hen does the spiritual biography of a person begin, and how is it shaped? By one's place of birth? Family? Education? Encounters with others? Coincidences? Divine intervention itself?

For a ten- or twelve-year-old child to decide for herself about matters of faith and church would have seemed amazing to those around her. Perhaps Magda was an especially sensitive, curious, and intelligent child. But above all she was an abandoned and desperate child.

And she now wanted and was expected to move from "heresy" to "truth," as Father Magri expressed it. The Catholic father, who was entrusted with the care of young souls, was not just any priest from the neighborhood. He was a highly regarded theologian as well as a famous commentator on Dante's *Divine Comedy*. Indeed, it was none other than the pastor of the Waldensian congregation, to which Grand-Maman belonged, who had recommended

Father Magri for this assignment of mentoring Magda after her decision to convert to Catholicism.

When Grand-Maman requested the right to accompany her granddaughter, Father Magri rejected the idea. From his perspective, Catholic teaching under the oversight of a Russian Orthodox-Waldensian made the whole project overly complicated.

Instead of taking place in a bright space in the church, Magda's catechism happened in a dismal, small sacristy. The damp room smelled musty and somewhat acidic, and Father Magri added further layers to the aroma with both his pipe and his peppermint candies. The large, handsome priest addressed his students in a friendly and polite tone, interrupted only by violent sneezing attacks triggered by the tobacco. Then the priest would take a large handkerchief into his large hands and loudly blow his large nose. For Magda, all of this triggered fear. Still more fear.

In this gloomy place, Magda also had her first confession, a so-called auricular confession: a recitation of one's sins in a confession booth in which the person confessing is heard but not seen. "And thus began the era of my scruples," she wrote later. "How does one make everything right and good? Truly good? And where is the border between good and evil? It was unbelievable how many sins there were! But which among them had I actually committed?"

Magda's family was preparing to celebrate her first Communion when an unexpected obstacle suddenly emerged. Magda was to receive Holy Communion not with the others, who came from lower economic classes, but rather in a mass celebrated by the Florentine archbishop. Both Father Magri and the archbishop thought Magda was sufficiently prepared, but then a simple, humble priest who had helped with the mass preparations expressed a concern: Had this young girl even received a legitimate baptism? In principle, Protestant baptisms were regarded as legitimate. But could anyone prove that Magda had been baptized with pure water and not, for example, with rosewater? The truth was that no one could actually prove this. And so, on the evening before her first Communion, Magda was baptized once again. And to ensure that no one could ever declare this baptism illegitimate, Magda was required to renounce her old faith—also in Latin—both before and after the event: "Renuntio!" But exactly whom or what was she renouncing? She could not have said, but the sound of this solemn and rather eerie word remained in her ear for the rest of her life: "Renuntio!"

The next morning, Magda received her first Holy Communion in the private chapel of the palace of the archbishop. Before the celebration, Magda endured a night filled with fear. Again and again she had confessed her sins—all the sins that she had learned in catechism, both venal and mortal. "If someone steals more than five lire, it is a mortal sin!" a child had told her. Magda had never stolen anything, but there were also sins that no one had noticed. She reviewed the sins of children and the sins of adults, even when she did not always know what the words describing the latter category meant. And then she imagined once again the moment in which the bishop would lay the host on her tongue. At that moment she dare not, under any circumstance, touch or bite it with her teeth. The host was Jesus himself, and she could not possibly chew Jesus into pieces! She had practiced with an unconsecrated wafer. But what if she did so nonetheless?

Morning came, the mass commenced, and the terrifying moment loomed closer. Now the bishop placed the host on her tongue. A cloth under her chin prevented crumbs from falling to the floor in the unlikely event that any bits broke loose. Everything went according to plan. The consecrated host was easy to swallow without chewing. "But . . . I felt nothing," Magda wrote later. "Absolutely nothing. The heavens failed to open. My spirit remained exactly the way it was, unsettled, full of expectations . . . disappointed. And now? Now? Nothing."

Magda's wish had been to be a fully normal Catholic girl—to no longer have to fear hell, and to simply belong. Soon after her first Communion, her father moved with his new family to Verona. Magda remained in Florence where, at the beginning of the 1914 school year, she entered another boarding school. It was a cloister school of the Mantellate Sisters, whose name could be traced to their distinctive long black veils. Here Magda was finally a Catholic among Catholics. For hours on end she prayed the Ave Maria, the Pater Noster, and the Gloria Patri, not out of piety but as a penitential practice. Her father confessor was strict, and Magda was even stricter with herself. Whereas her classmates entered the confessional booth, quickly murmured something, and left the church relieved and carefree, Magda agonized day and night, brooding on her fears. Were there sins that she had not yet confessed? Should she repeat the last prayer once more just to be sure? She had made a commitment, but now it surely was no longer valid.

As a convert, she had experienced a special grace. But now she needed to prove her worthiness; or, at least, that was how she saw it. So Magda was once again different from the rest—not one who had always been among the elect, but someone who needed to be eternally grateful that she had converted to the true path.

***

Around the same time, however, an entirely new theme loomed on the horizon. The summer of 1914 that transformed all of Europe began for Magda with an exciting trip. Finally she would meet the mysterious stranger, her grandfather Vladimir Wissotzky! No longer living "deep in Russia," Grand-Papa had moved to Wirballen, an important toll station on the German-Russian border crossing that is found today on the border between Lithuania and Russia. Grand-Papa was stationed there as a general and as the head of tariffs.

Grand-Maman undertook the journey with her three granddaughters—Lalli; Lalli's sister, Dudy; and Magda. The trip took them over the Alps and then from the southernmost part of Germany to its extreme north. It was an endlessly long train trip, which provided Grand-Maman enough time to explain to the children why they had never met their almost-mythical grandfather. As immigrants, he and Grand-Maman had lived with their three small children, first in Geneva and then in Florence. But even though they had quickly adapted to their new life, earning a living by teaching Russian and French and taking in other immigrants as boarders, Grand-Papa had always remained a foreigner. He never understood that being noble was not a profession in itself, Grand-Maman explained. Although they both had come from very privileged families, they now found themselves anonymous and in strained financial circumstances. "He was unhappy," Grand-Maman told her granddaughters. "He spent money that he didn't have. And then one day he decided to return to our old homeland." Grand-Maman concluded her explanation with a deep sigh.

She had allowed him to go, and from that point on she had lived a much more peaceful life. Now she would see him again, with three granddaughters in tow whom he knew only from letters.

The reception by Grand-Papa was a memorable production. Magda's memoirs, however, devote only a few lines to the topic. She did recall that their grandfather's uniform as a general was easily an equal to that of the Italian king; indeed, it exceeded that of the king. Directly after their grandfather greeted the young women, he explained that, regrettably, he could only wear a portion of all the medals and ribbons granted him, since there was not enough room on his chest to wear them all at the same time. And then Grand-Papa showed them a gold watch that was a gift from the czar himself.

There was little time for the travelers to be impressed with anything else, however—the news of the outbreak of war soon created a massive upheaval. Grand-Maman and her granddaughters quickly set about their return journey. If the prudent grandmother had not happened to have a few Austrian crowns in her luggage that she could produce at the train station in Berlin, they likely would have been prevented from continuing their journey. They managed to travel through Austria to Lindau, and from there to the Bodensee in Switzerland, and then to Florence.

A long journey had come to an end, and opportunities for travel that should have normally just begun for Magda were now clearly impossible. The war made the borders impassable, and the boarding school, whose high walls resembled a fortress, made Magda feel as if she were a prisoner during the years she was enrolled there. Three times a year she and the other students could receive visits from their parents, but her father seldom showed up during these rare opportunities. Did he have other worries during the war? Had he really forgotten his oldest daughter? Or did he blame her—consciously or unconsciously—for the death of his beloved first wife? In any case, he did not give much thought to Magda.

The time in which Magda languished at the Mantellate school—where she was trapped, underchallenged, and bored—included a year of preparation for the life of a lady. The possibility that a young woman like Magda might have interests entirely different from ironing lace or decorating a table occurred to no one. For five long years, Magda felt as if she had been pushed aside. What she was supposed to learn simply did not interest her, and she was not permitted to study the things that did. Moreover, the daily life of boarding school students was as rigorous and scheduled as a prison camp.

Nevertheless, Magda learned something decisive during these years. She learned how to find her way out of the fearful and depressive behavior of her childhood. Magda first became insolent, and then she became happy.

***

This may have begun one Saturday at confession.

"Your Reverence, I do not wish to make a confession," Magda began. On the other side of the confessional, the priest, made invisible by a curtain of heavy red cloth, remained silent for a moment.

"Why?" he then exclaimed. His voice was tinged with surprise and anger.

"Because I don't believe in it," said Magda as she started to leave.

"Wait!" said the priest. "Stay seated for a moment. I don't want others to see that you are not . . . well, you know what I mean. It would not be a good example for the others."

"Are you encouraging me to lie?" Now Magda was the angry one. "I don't need to pretend to be anything to my classmates. I've already told them that I'm not going to go to confession anymore. I refuse to lie to them about something like this!"

"I was becoming angry," Magda later recalled. "He wanted to save the souls of my classmates. I shouldn't infect them! He did all he could, and it instilled in me an evil sort of joy to see him trapped like a fly in a spider's nest. A dictator is always vulnerable, no matter if they base their claims on political or religious ideas."

Grand-Maman never knew that Magda was once again drawing close to the Protestant church—that she met secretly for conversations with the Waldensian pastor, and that, in the end, she formally renounced her membership in the Roman Catholic Church. Long after Grand-Maman's death, Magda continued to pay her grandmother's Waldensian church membership fee. She wanted to be sure that the name Varia Wissotzky remained on the membership roll, while she herself remained anonymous. "Freedom, freedom—after all of these difficulties," she wrote.

"In matters of religion, the beginning of my life was, well, bizarre," Magda reflected. "Orthodox? Protestant? Catholic? No religion at all? All this would be resolved in the future."

Still, where was she to turn? The mother church could never replace her own mother, a mother Magda had never known.

4

Fleeing the Cloister

Florence, 1918–25

The year that marked the end of World War I was also the year of the Spanish influenza, and the entire world fell victim. Twenty to forty thousand people died every day, from Accra to Berlin to Boston. In Florence, there had not been such a devastating pandemic since the Black Death of the fourteenth century. Grand-Maman now began to care for the sick in addition to her regular philanthropic activities. In contrast to many other influenza outbreaks, most of the victims of the 1918 flu were young adults. It was a year that Florentines would remember as the year from hell.

For Magda, however, 1918 was the year of her liberation—the year in which she fled the walls of the cloister and escaped from the shadows of the long dark curtains. In her hand she held not only a graduation certificate but also the national diploma of honor. With this document, she qualified for entrance into college and was the only one of her classmates to receive this honor. Several of her teachers had finally accepted—and even encouraged—the fact that the newly rebellious Magda occupied herself much more happily with thick books than with lace embroidery, as well as the fact that she still loved to read the *Divine Comedy*, even though she had nearly memorized it. Now a path had opened for her to the Istituto Superiore di Magistero, a teachers' college known for its high standards.

Italian universities had first admitted female students in 1876, but Florence was not among them. This had changed by the turn of the century, but the ambition of a young woman to study at a university was still quite exotic. Magda's dream was to pursue what we know today as social work. Grand-Maman had gone before her as an example, even if Magda hoped to do more than give poor children spoonfuls of cod liver oil or wipe the forehead of an influenza victim with a cool towel.

Actually, in childlike innocence and naiveté, Magda had already been doing social work for years. In light of Magda's later life, this foreshadowed what was to come. When Magda and her cousin Lalli were seven or eight years old, they established together a "charity society." Signora Bronconi had prompted the idea. This simple woman struggled to support herself by enclosing Chianti bottles in straw latticework done in the local style. And since she received only a meager wage for this, she supplemented her income by accompanying the two upper-class girls to school every morning. Naturally, she had no inkling what she had set in motion by making Magda and Lalli aware of the poor people who lived along the route to the school.

Encountering the needy had an immediate effect on the two sensitive girls. Already on the first day of school, Magda and Lalli knew what they had to do. Since the school did not supply a noon meal, the girls carried their picnic lunch in small willow baskets. During the afternoon break, they ate only half the food they had brought, and on the way home they gave the other half to a beggar they encountered at the Piazza Indipendenza. This first charitable deed had consequences. Within a few days, the number of people who came to regard the cousins as their "patrons" grew; soon the poor and needy were waiting for them not only in the Piazza Indipendenza but also elsewhere along the route. This required the girls to acquire more food.

But not only food. Soon the children of strangers were climbing up the iron door in front of the villa as Magda and Lalli offered them presents. The little girls with big hearts divested themselves of all kinds of things, including items that, strictly speaking, belonged to other members of the family. The only thing they didn't have to share was money, though they wished they did. This called for "professional" fundraising. And where should they collect money if not at school? They asked their classmates to contribute to their cause, and several of their fellow students generously donated a few lire.

Grand-Maman found the girls' collection of money, but it never occurred to her to ask where it had come from, so she sent the girls to the bakery to buy sandwiches with their donated funds. Tormented by their consciences and fully convinced that they were caught in an impossible, almost tragic situation, the two girls ate the sandwiches. How would they ever redeem themselves for this betrayal of both the poor and their fellow students?

At that point they came up with a new idea. Occasionally, a rag collector would come by their house. The girls could earn money by selling him clothes. And so the plan went forward. The ragman was delighted with the clothes they offered—neither he nor the generous benefactors were the least bit troubled that what they had pulled from the closet were clearly not rags. But as soon as they began to distribute the money, the number of children who begged them for small gifts grew. Still, Lalli and Magda did not run out of ideas. They began to dampen the clothes with water. After all, the clothes were sold by weight. If the clothes weighed more, they reasoned, they would also earn more. But the rag collector was not blind to these tricks, and with that their charitable society came to an end. The cousins interpreted this in a way that harmonized with their view of the world: it was God who had put an end to their deceit.

***

Now, as an adult, Magda was eager to further develop her impulse to help others. To do so, she needed to begin by helping herself. Her studies at the Istituto Superiore di Magistero were not only a pleasure but also a "lifesaver," as she later said, one that pulled her out of the profound constraints of her childhood. Things were not easy. Magda's father did not contribute any money to her tuition, food, or lodging, which meant she had to devote every spare moment to her tutoring job in order to meet her obligations. Because her lodgings did not include a bathroom, she was forced to use the shower in the public bathhouse. Whenever she needed a break she went to the YWCA (Young Women's Christian Association), which was more comfortable than her own home, if one could call her solitary room a "home."

Magda enjoyed her time as a student, and she was an extraordinarily successful one. So when the college offered her the opportunity to do a further degree in French, Magda jumped at the opportunity. By the end, she left the Istituto with two certificates, one from the Italian college and another that bore the seal of the University of Grenoble. Even though Magda had never been to France, her French, according to her certification, was superb. At the time, no one could have guessed just how important the seal of a French university would be for her one day.

So what could a well-educated, pretty Florentine woman in her early twenties actually do? Magda was dating a man who, she soon came to realize, was harboring extremely serious intentions—unfortunately, Magda thought. He was Belgian and was a strict Catholic who worked at the American Express office in Florence. He was not interested in open-ended flirting but spoke instead of marriage and raising Catholic children. Magda struggled to gain more time. Falkenberg was clearly a handsome man; and Magda liked him well enough. But he was so serious—and she had only recently discovered her freedom!

Magda allowed her imagination to run wild. She made plans for the future. She dreamed of a big trip. The trip of Magda's dreams pointed to America. Her classmates had told her about opportunities to study social work in New York City—postgraduate courses for women who had already completed their degrees. She now fit into that category. The only question remaining was how she would organize and finance the plan.

The first thing she did was take a job. Her job, which she accepted near the end of her studies, was extremely pleasant. Magda accompanied a young woman who was traveling for pleasure in Florence and the surrounding region. Miss Wilcox, a wealthy American from New Hampshire, was living for a few months in Florence. Hoping to combine pleasure with practical matters, she had been looking for a local, culturally informed traveling companion who could join her for museum visits and parties while also teaching her a little Italian. Magda was the ideal candidate. With her cheerful multilingual chatter, she enlivened their travels. Miss Wilcox was so taken with Magda that she soon expanded their excursions into short trips, moving beyond visits to Fiesole and other standard destinations close to Florence. Thus the two women extended their tours all the way to Lago Maggiore and to Zermatt, Switzerland.

There, at a post office in Zermatt, Magda found a letter awaiting her: the New York School of Social Work was welcoming her to join them as a student in the coming academic year. Not only that, but Magda would also receive a stipend from her new school!

Her joy was boundless. The fulfillment of a grand dream was suddenly within reach. However, that exhilaration was soon dampened when she discovered that only a few months earlier, the U.S. government had introduced new quotas for immigrants from southern and eastern Europe. Only visitors from northern and western Europe could enter without restrictions. Florence was considered to be in the south, even though most Italians, then as now, regarded themselves as northern European.

But an immigration quota is not the same thing as a ban on entering the county. As Magda was hoping and worrying, Miss Wilcox came up with a good idea: "How would it be if you accompanied me on my return voyage to New York? We could continue our Italian lessons on board." Thus, the future New York student would initially travel as a teacher—thereby resolving the question of the trip itself.

***

Magda's departure from Florence happened so easily that it was bittersweet. There were so few people in Florence whom Magda would miss. Grand-Maman was dead; her father, Oscar, had retreated long ago; and her relationship with her stepmother had never been a close one. All that remained were Sunday acquaintances. Only Falkenberg, the earnest Belgian banker, insisted on accompanying Magda not just to the train station but to the harbor as well.

But only one goodbye remained imprinted in Magda's memory for the rest of her life. A few days before her departure, Magda visited the grave of her mother. There she stood in the shadows of the tall cypress trees and read what her father had chiseled into the stone.

> *Nelly Wissotzky*
> *morta a ventitre anni*
> *Il 29 novembre 1901*
> *appena divenuta madre*
> *e da solo dieci mesi sposa.*
> *Anima eletta, purissima,*
> *sbocciata come fiore*
> *che morendo dà il frutto.*
> *Oggi, riposa nella pace divina*
> *ove attende l'inconsolabile marito*
> *Oscar Grilli*
> *per no lasciarlo più*

Nelly Wissotzky
died at the age of 23
on November 29, 1901,
only shortly after she had become a mother
and married for scarcely ten months.
Elected soul, purer than pure,
like a bud that blossoms,
brings forth fruit, and dies.
She rests in divine peace,
where she awaits her heartbroken husband,
Oscar Grilli,
where she will never leave him again.

That chiseled stone had stood there for nearly twenty-five years, and it had determined the life course of Magda's father. His wife—the first one, the "real one"—was a divine being, and this fact had shaped the life of his daughter. But now it was time for

Magda—who was completely of this earth, who was practical, pragmatic, and full of life—to leave this part of her world behind and to visit a country that suited her better. America was the land of those who looked to the future, who grasped for it, who were capable of happiness even if they didn't have two thousand years of cultural history behind them, and who were indifferent to a family history that had entangled Magda for almost a quarter of a century.

Marseille—Genoa—Naples—Palermo—New York. The French Fabre Line steamship made the trip in two weeks. Magda boarded in Naples, where Miss Wilcox was awaiting her. Magda had dreamed of a much longer passage by ship, with stops at unknown islands along the way. She thought that she would see people and animals that were completely different from all that she had known in Italy. But the rapid journey in a ship filled with poor emigrants from southern Italy who were desperate for a change in fortune was not exactly romantic. Nevertheless, she had received the ticket as a gift. And the ship was heading in the right direction.

PART II

5

A Piety Lacking Mercy

Saint-Quentin, France, 1901–10

The house where André Trocmé was born was only a few meters from the Champs-Elysées. That sounds more magnificent than it actually was, for the grand avenue in Paris is not the only Champs-Elysées in France. One of the main streets in Saint-Quentin, an industrial city not far from the Belgian border in northern France, has the same name.

The city is situated not far from the Somme, a river whose name still awakens bleak memories of World War I. Already during the Wars of Religion, more than three hundred years before André's birth, Saint-Quentin played a significant role as a border town.[1] In those days the borders between Catholic and Protestant territories mattered a great deal. Protestant weavers fled here from the Catholic Netherlands, bringing with them not only their Protestant hymnals but also their mastery of a particular craft: the weaving of fine cloth. Ever since, the history of the city has been

1 The French Wars of Religion, sometimes known as the Huguenot Wars, were periods of fighting between Roman Catholics and Huguenots (Reformed, or Calvinist, Protestants) in the sixteenth century.

shaped by the textile industry, including, centuries later, the life of the Trocmé family. Paul Trocmé, André's father, was a true son of the city—a Protestant and a third-generation proprietor of a textile factory. The prosperity of the family was rooted in fine lace and wool, which the family not only produced but also marketed very successfully to wealthy customers in Paris.

So even if the Champs-Elysées in Saint-Quentin was only a pale imitation of the "real" Champs-Elysées, the Trocmé family home was still quite impressive. Not counting the kitchen and the servant quarters, it had eighteen rooms, twelve of which were bedrooms. The family was rich in children as well as possessions: seven sons and two daughters populated the house, even though the difference in their ages was such that they never all lived in the house at the same time. By the time the last child was born, the first grandchild had already appeared. Because André, the youngest, was born on the morning of Easter Sunday, he was given a second name—Pascal, the Easter child. In photographs, he can be identified by the long blond curls that fell to his shoulders.

All of this may make it sound as if André had a carefree childhood in the cheerful company of many siblings. Unfortunately, the truth was quite different. "It was not a happy home," André wrote in his memoirs. He described the nearby Champs-Elysées as "the big melancholy promenade."

What was so oppressive about life in this grand house with its spacious garden? "I was raised in the strict religious environment of a Huguenot family," André wrote. "More than anything else in the world, my father valued the concept of duty. From the time I was very young, I learned to hate all bad things: not the bad things I saw in other people, but the bad things that I did myself."

***

There was, for example, the story of the butter cookies. It happened during a time in which it was fully normal for adults to eat treats while the children looked on, wide-eyed, yearning for the day when they too would be old enough to enjoy such delicacies. André's father had a custom of drinking coffee after the noon meal while savoring a Petit Beurre—a simple, timeless butter cookie. Paul Trocmé then ate a second butter cookie in the evening with his tea.

Except for these occasions, the cookie jar always sat high up in the kitchen cupboard. On several occasions just before bedtime, André smuggled one or two of these cookies from the jar into his bedroom, where he hid them under his pillow. When Pierre, a brother with whom André shared the bedroom, fell asleep, André would carefully pull a cookie out from under the pillow and eat it.

One day André was summoned to appear before his father. A servant had discovered a slightly chewed and crumbling cookie in André's bed. Undoubtedly, he had fallen asleep in the midst of his evil deed.

"Is it true that you steal cookies?" his father asked.

"No, it wasn't me," replied André, sick with fear.

"How, then, can it be that a cookie was found in your bed?"

"Maybe somebody put it there," André lied, for a second time.

The identity of that "somebody" became clear to André's father. Madeleine, André's much older sister, lived in the house with her small son, Jean. Jean was a temperamental rascal who always got on his grandfather's nerves.

"Well then," his father said to the servant, "you must believe André. He never lies."

Later, André sat paralyzed in his room as he listened to the screams of little Jean being whipped by his grandfather in the next room. As André recalled many years later, the incident was followed by weeks of deathly fear.

I now knew that I was considered to be an honest young man who never lied. But I also knew that I was not worthy of this trust. The shame overwhelmed me—the shame of being regarded as someone who I was not. I knew—and this was the cause of still more pain—that I would never have the courage to admit to my cowardice. I was too cowardly to acknowledge my own cowardice. I looked into the abyss of sin and became a deeply unhappy young boy, constantly blushing and always thinking that I saw an accusation in the eyes of others when they looked at me. As a consequence, I always looked down.

But why couldn't André speak with his father, even weeks and months afterward? And why was there no other person in the house to whom he could have turned? And how was it possible that a child of his age could conclude that a cookie jar was so closely associated with the abyss of sin, and that this could lead to such profound self-contempt?

Perhaps this can best be explained by the particular kind of Protestant rigor, not at all unusual at the time, that set the tone in the Trocmé home. It was an earnest faith, but one lacking in mercy—a piety that did not recognize forgiveness or grace. Every small sin could be the first step on a path that led to the abyss. Therefore, every sin must be resisted without compromise.

***

Both sides of the Trocmé family, the maternal as well as the paternal, had descended from French Huguenots, even though André's mother was German. Paul Trocmé was first married to Marie Walbaum, who died at the age of forty-four after the birth of her ninth child. His second wife, Paula Schwerdtmann, a teacher from a small village in Germany, was the daughter of a Lutheran pastor. She and Paul had two more children—Pierre and André.

André's father, Paul Trocmé, and mother, Paula Schwerdtmann Trocmé. Private collection.

Since two children from Paul Trocmé's first marriage had died, the Trocmé family totaled nine children.

André always treasured his memories of visits with his grandparents in Germany. The elderly couple were earnest, unshakable churchgoing people living in a classic German parsonage. Here André was happy—the coffee breaks! the sweet rolls! his grandfather seated in the wingback chair smoking his enormous pipe! Here André experienced a cozy, pious life that was refreshing. And not only André, who had always been somewhat anxious, but also his mother, who traveled with him. The warm world of the little village was a soothing contrast to the cold atmosphere of his paternal home.

Back in Saint-Quentin, André's mother transformed once again into the strict matron of a big house. The children were required to address her as "Mère," in contrast to the older half siblings, who had addressed their mother as "Maman." The corsage of the large, stout woman was tightly bound; her hair was fixed snugly in a bun on the back of her head. Her glasses, in the pince-nez style, did nothing to soften the contours of her face.

All practical matters regarding the children were the responsibility of the nannies, Jeanne and Marie. It was a nanny who wiped noses, bandaged scraped knees, and above all, ensured that the children conducted themselves appropriately in every setting. Nonetheless, in the evenings after Jeanne or Marie had bathed the two little ones and put them to bed, *la mère* would often appear to sing with her sons and to read books. She was the one who taught them to read independently at a very young age. The aura of their mother was something special—her presence lent a sparkle to at least a few special hours of the week.

***

The strictly ordered world of the Trocmé family was shattered on June 24, 1911. It was a sunny Saturday at the beginning of summer. The Trocmé parents had spent the night with the younger children in the family's country house in Saint-Gobain, some thirty kilometers (twenty or so miles) south of their home in the city. Now they were planning on returning to Saint-Quentin, but the weather was simply too beautiful to take the most direct route.

Paul Trocmé took enormous pleasure in offering his wife—along with Pierre, André, and his wife's niece—a ride in his new car. It was a 1910 Panhard et Levassor, a vehicle that marked the pinnacle of progress and elegance in the automotive world of the day. The rear of the car, occupied by the children, was enclosed. Both front seats, by contrast, were in the open as in a convertible, protected in the front by a partial windshield and shaded by a roof that extended from the rear. Madame Trocmé sat in the passenger seat during this little excursion through the tall cornfields and the blooming meadows while Monsieur took in hand the steering wheel.

It was a heavenly trip until a smaller vehicle passed them, enshrouding them in a plume of dust. Who would do such a thing? And who would think that they could drive faster than a Panhard et Levassor? Paul Trocmé pressed his foot on the gas. He would soon make it clear that a luxury limousine was not going to be insulted by a pile of junk. The children in the back seat screamed with joy. "You show him, Papa!"

"And then it happened," wrote André in his memoirs.

The thing that had been predestined from the beginning: that Papa would be the death of my mother. Since then I too have died a hundred, yes, a thousand times, through this accident. A horrified little circle of five human beings seized by the terror of death. Something, like an enormous hammer—but where did it come from?—smashed us. Immeasurably enormous and brutal, while simultaneously so ironic and so distant. *It*, that thing that we call death and yet is no one—not even a skeleton with sufficient awareness to at least have a conversation. *It*, a nothing, had utterly destroyed us, ground us up and then left us lying there in the mangled metal. There was no sound except for the crickets chirping in the meadow and the gasoline that was slowly dripping out of the gas tank. . . . I died a thousand times with my mother.

Then the first movement, groaning, crawling on the ground. This horrifying effort to escape from death's grasp. Trembling, the three small children and Papa, holding his broken wrist, gathered themselves alongside the wreckage. And then they began to laugh like maniacs simply because they were still living.

Only then did one of us notice Mother. No, even then it was clear that it was no longer her. On the street ten meters behind us lay a large body covered in dust. Her legs were spread slightly apart; a ribbon of blood ran out of the right side of her mouth.

The eyes were closed. Not closed as if in sleep, but like a window of a house that has been abandoned for a very long time. On the face an expression of absence, the mark of It, of nothingness. The nervous laughter of the survivors now shifted into silent sobbing, jaws clenched in order not to scream and to keep from trembling.

A doctor. A taxi, which appeared out of nowhere. And suddenly, in one devastating blow, in a single scream, I understood everything. It all became clear: I no longer had a mother. My whole body ached—my heart, my soul—and I was reborn. I was a man.

6

This Whole
Isolated World

Saint-Quentin, 1911–14

The funeral service took place in the home itself. "I killed her! I killed her!" Again and again André's father interrupted the service with his despairing cry.

For the family, the mother had died in the dust on the street. By medical definition, she died in bed, wrapped in white linen cloth, a few days later. The dying woman's bed was right outside André's bedroom, and for three long nights the boy had heard the irregular gasping breath of his mother through the wall. Then the neighboring room suddenly fell silent. Yet the gasps of his mother continued to resound in André's ears long after she had ceased to breathe.

André was ten years old.

***

In his first year without a mother, André's favorite pastime was "playing army."

"You're dead!"

"No, I'm not! My cannonball hit you before you shot me!"

Together with Étienne—who, as a son of André's half sister, was André's nephew even though the two boys were the same age—André transformed the garden into a battlefield. The two boys merged everything they knew about war into a wild game. At school they had begun reading about Caesar's wars in Gaul; then came a few stories of Napoleon in winter right outside Moscow; and then things that their father—or grandfather, in Étienne's case—had told them about the Franco-German War of 1870–71, which he had personally experienced as a soldier forty years earlier. An old wooden chest, with the help of a strong rubber band, was transformed into a catapult. The white gravel from the driveway provided a rich source of munitions. And finally, taking note of a completely new development in real life, the boys folded and glued fighter planes out of paper.

A harmless amusement? An imaginative opportunity to simply let off steam? Surely it was both, at least until the summer of 1912, one year after the death of his mother, when André had an experience while playing army that turned a little ruffian into a reflective young man.

The Trocmé garden was completely isolated from the outside world by a fence and tall trees. The gardener who tended this paradise did not enter through the house but rather through a small door on one of the garden's narrow sides. One day the door stood open because the gardener had left without locking it. Étienne and André were imitating cannon fire and playing war games so boisterously that the sound of their play could be heard on the street. Suddenly, they were interrupted by the creaking of the gate. A strange man stood there, wearing a cap that shrouded his pale, yellowed face. A cigarette dangled from the corner of his mouth. Broad suspenders secured his pants. He was obviously a vagrant. The man looked at the house. Then his gaze swept across the garden and he stared at the boys. He looked at them for a long time without saying a word. Then, with a bitter mocking laugh, he said, "Tas d'cons" (A bunch of idiots). He turned around and carefully closed the garden door behind him.

For André, what could have merely been a harmless interruption of their game became a decisive life experience, one marked by the sudden realization that there were people outside the enclosed green kingdom of his family who were quite different from him. Usually, they were hidden from view. But when such people suddenly appeared, it was possible for them not to feel envy and wonder when considering the lives of the Trocmés. They could turn and walk away, regarding everything they saw—the house, the garden, the games, this whole isolated world—as idiotic. Was it possible that there were people out there who thought entirely differently than he did? And was it possible that some of them might even despise his family's lifestyle?

The desire to continue with the war games evaporated. What's more, from that moment forward, André would always feel as if he were being watched and judged by an outside court of opinion, even when there was nobody around. "The pale vagrant" became a fixed image that haunted and unsettled him for a long time—until he befriended the image. "It was a very good thing that this vagrant thought I was an idiot. He has become part of the secret inner circle of my mind, almost like a family member," wrote André as an adult. He confessed that he sometimes even engaged in conversation with the man.

Come, pale vagrant, why don't you rest awhile until I call you again. You have shown me that there are battles unfolding among the social classes, and for that I am very grateful to you. Without knowing it, you did me a very good deed when you expressed such disdain for our world. "Tas d'cons." I had not known this expression—you were the one who taught it to me, and since then I have often whispered it to myself when I had to deal with ridiculous people who had absolutely no idea about the people around them.

***

At the end of the summer of his mother's death, André was sent to school. Until then, tutors had instructed him at home. His mother had taught him to read; various women in the household taught French grammar and piano (which he soon gave up because of a clear lack of talent). For all remaining subjects he had visited the director of an elementary school. Now he was heading to the lycée, a college-preparatory school that had not changed in the slightest since his father had attended in the mid-1850s. French, English, Latin, math, history, and geography were still the subjects for ten-year-olds. Rhetoric, philosophy, and German were added later. The pedagogy was driven by memorization, fixed rules of analysis and commentary, copying, testing, and repetition. Outwardly disciplined but mentally disengaged, André sat, bored, at his desk.

André was thirteen years old and enjoying summer vacation at the family home in Saint-Gobain when World War I erupted. Of course, it did not erupt like a volcano, from whose heat and ashes there is no escape. It was, instead, a consequence of numerous political decisions and policies that had consciously calculated the risks of war. For the Trocmés, however, the war overwhelmed them as if a natural catastrophe. The family returned to the city, which was already swarming with soldiers. The mobilization was fully under way. France and Germany had been at war for three weeks by then, and the front line was not on German soil but already in neighboring Belgium.

All kinds of thoughts raced through André's mind, even as he consciously tried to give the appearance of being a level-headed young man. Were the Germans, whom people now regarded with contempt and loathing, the same people he had met during his visits to his grandparents' home in Petzen? Were they people like his grandparents, his uncles and aunts, his cousins, or the children with whom he had swum in the river close to Braunschweig? Did they include friendly and sympathetic people like the governesses who had come into the Trocmé home after the death of his mother?

No, that couldn't be! The Germans whom the French were now justly fighting must be completely different. They had a spike on their helmeted heads; they obeyed an emperor who was an unbearable fraud; they set fires to people's homes, shot innocent civilians, hacked off the hands of children—everyone knew this! Yet no one he had come to know in the home of his mother's parents would have done such things. These Germans must be a completely different sort of people.

And yet a nagging doubt persisted in André's mind. What would he do if someday he encountered his cousin Wilhelm—who was, by now, of the age to be conscripted into the army—and Wilhelm was wearing the uniform of a German soldier?

When the front advanced to only thirty kilometers (nineteen miles) from Saint-Quentin and the thunder of the cannons could be heard day and night, André had an idea. He would serve as an intermediary between the Germans and the French. When Germans marched into Saint-Quentin, he would stand before them and talk with them in German. Why else had he been learning this language from the time of his childhood? He would tell them that they should not destroy the city and that they were not permitted to shoot its inhabitants. His sign would be a white flag. Just as Rahab of the Old Testament had saved her family by dangling a red rope on the walls of Jericho, so he, André, would save the city of Saint-Quentin from destruction with his white flag.

Now, all he needed was a white flag. The flag, which he found in the attic, was the blue, white, and red flag of France, known as the Tricolore. No matter. For years it had enjoyed a place of honor on July 14, Bastille Day, and it had the great advantage of already being a flag. This was much more practical than sewing a flag himself and somehow affixing it to a flagpole.

Time was pressing. André took the flag, climbed to the top of an apple tree in the garden, and tied it to a branch. Blue, white, red. It looked wonderful!

***

"Who did that!" In the *petit salon*, the small parlor where the extended family gathered for tea, there was great excitement.

"It was me!" André stepped forward, proud to acknowledge his deed. For the past month, the fate of the fatherland was the primary topic of conversation in the *petit salon*. But everyone else had only talked; he alone had actually done something.

"Are you crazy?" "A flag like that is a provocation!" "You are going to unleash German rage!" "You are putting your own head at risk—and ours!" "Climb immediately up the tree and bring that thing down!" Everyone was talking at the same time.

The Tricolore had lost. Disappointed, André did as he was told.

New rumors were circulating when he awoke the next morning. It was not the Germans but the English who were at the city gates. The Germans had been surrounded and forced into retreat. At five in the afternoon a British regiment was supposed to march into the city. As if in a festive parade, the soldiers marched in majestic pomp and splendor through the boulevard. André ran along the streets to greet the victors. He even thought he heard bagpipes. But then came a scream, and a wild retreat of the spectators. "It's the Germans!"

André raced back to the house. He wanted to be the first to give the *petit salon* the horrific news. But the parlor, like all the other rooms in the house, was empty. The whole family had already fled into the basement. Everyone, that is, except for his father, who must have been somewhere outside.

André sat alongside the others, wondering whether he was a coward. Through the basement window, he could hear a door being broken down in the neighbor's house. Someone had shot at the advancing troops. Loud voices. Gunshots.

At the time, André had no idea that, as they were sitting there, a German patrol had forced his father to act as a human shield. From one street corner to the next, soldiers had pushed André's father ahead of them to prevent French defenders from shooting at them. Their plan succeeded. Neither the soldiers nor André's father were injured, though it is possible that only his body escaped unscathed.

The next day the German flag flew from all public buildings. What a humiliation. For the next four-and-a-half years, the German flag would fly on those masts. For André they awakened a single desire: *liberté*—freedom!

7

The Man without a Face

Saint-Quentin, 1914–17

At the beginning, the war seemed to André to be a bit like games at summer camp. André, his brother Pierre, and his nephew Étienne regarded the first weeks of the war as if they were a sports contest, and they found opportunities at every hand to create adventures, small and large.

It all started with an effort to create a collection of posters. The Germans communicated their orders in the form of placards, which they affixed to trees, fences, and walls. Sometimes the posters contained commands to the city's inhabitants; sometimes they announced executions. The three boys made a game of getting up early in the morning before school, just as dawn was breaking, to rip down the placards or, even better, to remove them carefully and hide them away as part of a growing pile of placards they were collecting. Once or twice, one of the boys was seen by a German soldier. But since the boys could run faster—and since they knew all the alleys of the old city better than the occupiers—they were able to escape their pursuers.

The second passion of the Trocmé boys was to collect shrapnel from grenades—naturally, the larger the better. Sadly, there were plenty of opportunities to find shrapnel. The very thing that caused so much fear and terror for those around them—the noise of an exploding grenade—held a special appeal for the carefree, self-declared avengers of the fatherland. Since the Germans considered the train station at Saint-Quentin to be a strategic transportation hub for people and supplies, it was often the focus of Allied reconnaissance planes. Twice the station had come under intense bombardment. The munitions, loaded on trains from Germany, exploded—roofs were laid bare, windows shattered, strong walls cracked. And there were fatalities. The boys ran straight to the scene. The second attack on the train station nearly cost them their lives. A large chunk of plaster came crashing down from a house and missed them by a hair. Nonetheless, André, Pierre, and Étienne returned home from their expedition with several valuable finds, at least in their eyes, and they felt wonderful.

André had an especially challenging trophy in mind. He dreamed of finding a German spiked helmet and hiding it. Then, after the victory over the enemy, he would proudly show it off to his classmates. But that idea came to naught, and one day even the poster collection needed to disappear quickly. The three boys rolled up their posters, stuck them in bottles, and buried them in a distant corner of the garden. Years later someone discovered that the posters had survived the war intact, whereas the family's silverware and china, which were buried nearby, had fallen victim to a grenade.

***

The greatest adventure, however, was the announcement of the liberation of Saint-Quentin. Countless rumors had circulated throughout the city, most of them awakening hopes that were

quickly dashed. This prompted an idea for André and Pierre: using a small typewriter, they typed several copies of a leaflet. The
text was verbose and melodramatic, with many corrections. But
posted at the bottom was the line "Signed by General Joseph
Joffre." Joffre was a young hero who had already been victorious
in Vietnam, Timbuktu, and Madagascar. Surely he would soon
turn the fate of France in a positive direction. Adding his name to
the leaflets gave them a sense of official authorization.

"Citizens of Saint-Quentin!" the boys wrote. "In just a few
days the hour of your liberation will be at hand. After an in-
vincible offensive, the victorious forces of the Republic will raise
the banner of the fatherland over your courthouse . . ." And so
it went. The two propagandists pulled the pages from the typewriter and wrote in their own hand at the bottom: "Distributed
from 3,000 meters in the sky, signed: Moreau, Lieutenant of the
Airforce." Then they waited until dusk and scanned the skies. A
few minutes after they spotted a French airplane, they distributed
the leaflets throughout the abandoned streets.

The success was enormous. Before the boys left for school the
next morning, the butcher's son stood at the door, waving a leaflet
in his hand and calling out, "This time it's true! They're coming!"

It was the same at school: "Have you read it?" "General Joffre!
It's unbelievable!" Students and teachers alike celebrated with joy.
A family by the name of Moreau was already claiming that they
recognized the handwriting of their son in the signature at the
bottom of the flyer.

André and Pierre had to fake their happiness; all they felt was
anxiety. How could it be so easy to fool even adults? Only one
person remained unconvinced—André's father. "If General Joffre
was preparing an offensive, then he obviously wouldn't announce
it to the Germans," his father said. "And look at this affected style
of writing—it's absurd!"

Secretly, the boys were proud of their intelligent father. But they didn't offer a word of response regarding his doubts.

The incident came to naught. The offensive did not happen, the German flag continued to fly above the roof of the courthouse, and no one admitted that they had allowed themselves to be fooled.

Only weeks later did André and Pierre acknowledge to their father that they had concocted the whole lousy scheme. He didn't believe them.

***

But then came the year of 1916. Now even a child could not regard the war as just another adventure. Four dead people per square meter—that was the outcome of the Battle of Verdun. The battle lasted ten months; in the end, it resulted in no meaningful change in the location of the front.

The Battle of the Somme, which raged the same year, brought the war even closer to the Trocmés. Saint-Quentin was only thirty-five kilometers (twenty-two miles) from the site of the worst fighting, and the artillery fire could be heard day and night. On July 1, 1916, the first day of the battle, eight thousand young men died in the first half hour alone. Five months later, flamethrowers were invented, the first tanks were deployed, and airplanes were equipped with bombs. The result of the Battle of the Somme: one million deaths. No victory on either side.

For five long months, German reserve troops marched through Saint-Quentin, a mirror image of the movement of the wounded being transported in the opposite direction. Young men who had set out for the Western Front with boundless enthusiasm now lay bleeding in carts returning to field hospitals in the east. They were still the lucky ones, since there were also days in which no prisoners were taken and none of the injured were spared.

Three of André's half brothers fought on the French side: Robert, Eugène, and Maurice. Robert, closest in age to André and the one whom André idealized to the point of idolatry, was a captain in the infantry and was wounded. The Germans thought he was dead and left him lying in the filth. Robert, however, managed to save himself by crawling across the battlefield back to the French line. He was considered a war hero, and at the end of the war he had the honor of being one of the first French officers to march into liberated Brussels.

Given that his mother was German, André also had cousins who served in the German army and who marched through Saint-Quentin as German soldiers. He did not see them personally, but he heard about them later. Thus, at age fifteen, André knew people on both sides. He knew all of them to be upright, earnest, and conscientious men who were convinced they were serving a righteous cause.

***

Then came a brief moment—a scene that André witnessed on the street—that became for him another pivotal experience. It was a "revelation of the horrors of war," as he described it.

All of Saint-Quentin had been transformed into a hospital. As I was coming from the train station I encountered a group of wounded Germans. There was almost no transportation left, neither cars nor horses, so everyone who could still somehow manage to walk had to travel by foot to the field hospital that had been assigned to him. Three men were walking ahead of the group; all of them were injured and bandaged. The middle one had a huge ball, made of bandaging material, where his head should have been. He was not able to see, and he walked unevenly and could only remain standing with the help of his colleague. As he came nearer, I noticed with horror that he was missing his lower jaw. The bottom part of his face was nothing more than a wad of bandages pressed together and stained dark red from the blood. For a moment I felt as if I was having a heart attack. I had never known that *this* is what war was.

One thing was clear: I could not hate this man without a face. Saddened and horrified, I went back home.

A few days later André met a German soldier in the stairway of his house. There were German soldiers quartered at the Trocmé home.

The soldier stopped, looked at André in a friendly way, and grasped his arm. "Are you hungry?" the soldier asked. With a somewhat hesitant gesture, he offered the boy a piece of dark bread. The way he offered it to André suggested that the soldier was aware that the offer might be embarrassing.

"No," André answered in German. In the first place, the Trocmés were not going hungry. Second, he had no interest in eating dark German bread, which reportedly was made from potatoes. And third, even if he had been hungry, he never would have allowed a German to give him bread.

"No," said André brusquely. "I don't accept any bread from an enemy."

"I'm not your enemy," replied the soldier.

"Yes, you are," André responded quickly. "You are my enemy. You are wearing this uniform, and it's possible that tomorrow you will kill my brother. He is fighting against you so that we can finally be rid of you. Why did you come here in the first place?"

"I'm not the kind of person that you think." The soldier remained friendly. "I'm a Christian. Do you believe in God?"

André hesitated. For some time now he had been attending a gathering called the Union—the Union chrétienne de jeunes gens. It was a group of young men from the Protestant church, and he had become an enthusiastic member. Were there such groups in Germany? "I met Christ when I was in Breslau," the soldier told him. "I've given my life to him."

The two of them stood for a long time in the stairwell, and the German, named Kindler, spoke at great length about his conversion and his experiences with faith. The things that Kindler said touched André deeply.

"God has shown us that a Christian may not kill, ever," the German said. "We do not carry any weapons."

"But you are a soldier here!" André exclaimed.

"I spoke with my captain, and he sent me to the telegraph corps. Normally, field messengers carry a pistol or a knife with them. But I don't carry either. I have often been in danger between the lines, but then I sing a song or I pray. If God chooses to save my life, then he will do so. If not . . ."

For the first time in his life, André had encountered a man who refused military service for reasons of conscience—a person who would later be called a conscientious objector. If his conversation partner had been French, the news probably would have enraged him—"What? Aren't you willing to defend the fatherland that has been invaded and that people are now trampling underfoot?"

But the person here was a German. André felt respect, even esteem, for his behavior. This man was a Christian, perhaps a genuine, true Christian—the kind of person that he, along with all Christians, were meant to be.

***

The friendship with Kindler that developed over the next few days prompted all of André's ideals of nationalism and militarism to evaporate into thin air, and he experienced an enormous sense of release. This was the solution to the contradiction that had torn him apart. It was not the French who were fighting for God and country, but neither was it the Germans or the British. No one was! "I suddenly saw the war as it really was," André wrote. "A horrifying chaos in which everyone, including those who were directing the war, were criminals or victims. Each of them refused obedience to God in their own way in that they pretended to create justice in his name and with the help of cannons."

With great innocence and enthusiasm, André soon took the pious soldier to a meeting of the Union. The young men gaped when he introduced the German. Some could barely grasp what was happening and looked at André as if he were completely crazy. André translated what Kindler said, and when the German taught the French a canon, a song text with no other words than *hallelujah* and *amen*, the ice was broken.

At the end of the evening, everyone knelt for prayer, as was their custom. In the distance the battery shelling could be heard. Only a few kilometers away from their gathering, French and German troops were trying their best to kill one another. And then André, for the first time in his life, prayed out loud and in front of people who were listening to him. There was only one kingdom of God for all human beings—this much was suddenly and completely clear to him. And this kingdom was not something distant but rather something that, at that moment, felt tangible and close at hand.

***

A few days later Kindler was forced to go to the front. Before he departed, he invited André into his room and gave him a number of papers, a few photos, a pair of pliers, and a roll of electrical tape.

"Keep an eye on them until I return," he asked of André. "You will know when my regiment marches through Saint-Quentin on the journey home. If I am not part of the group, then I have either been wounded, captured, or killed. If I am wounded or captured, I'll have a message sent to you. If you hear nothing from me . . . God will know when the right time has come for him to take me to himself. If that should happen, please send these things to my wife. I have written down her address for you."

André never heard from Kindler again. Eventually, he packed the items and sent the package to Breslau.

In February 1917, the inhabitants of Saint-Quentin were evacuated. The city had become uninhabitable. The Trocmé textile factory had been ransacked long ago. To obtain parts made of copper, German soldiers had destroyed all the looms. There was no longer any reason why the Trocmé family should put their lives at risk in Saint-Quentin. The family needed to find a new place of refuge, somewhere as far from the front as possible.

8

Such a Thing as Beauty

Brussels, 1917–Paris, 1925

A wealthy man who had never walked down the boulevard without a formal coat. Two governesses who had never left the house without hat and gloves. A row of children who, from the time they first learned to walk, had been instructed, "Never forget that you are a Trocmé!" They had now become refugees pulling handcarts in the direction of the train station. They began a trek that fully eliminated every sort of social distinction. The small village near Brussels that they hoped to reach by train was not too far away, but in February, under these circumstances, the 150-kilometer (over ninety-mile) journey took an eternity. The mood of the exiles was subdued, but not without a sense of comfort and hope. An enormous treasure still remained in the Trocmés' possession that no war could ever take away: their far-flung network of relatives, acquaintances, friends, and friends of friends.

Indeed, this network was strong enough to deflect the worst of the difficulties that lay ahead for the Trocmé family. The war would come to an end a year and a half later, and although André

was a refugee child, one among many, the family network buff-
ered André and his family from much of the trauma experienced
by others. After André's family was driven from Saint-Quentin,
he attended the Jesuit school in Marcq, Belgium—by far the
most prestigious college-preparatory school in the region. He
lived on the generous mercy of distant relatives. Beginning in
August 1917, his family lived in an upper-class suburb of Brussels
in a temporarily abandoned banker's apartment, which a member
of the Belgian royal court had granted them. André traveled in
the very best circles, but every coin in his pocket had been loaned
to him. Although he was a large, almost heavyset, seventeen-year-
old, he was still extremely shy and apt to turn red at every moment. He found this life exhausting in the extreme. So he was
delighted when, in December 1918, the family moved to Paris to
begin, so he hoped, a new, somewhat normal life.

The journey took them past Saint-Quentin. The town was
almost completely destroyed. The Trocmé house had served to
quarter German officers, transforming an upper-middle-class
home into a combination of a robbers' den and a pig stall.
André's father already understood that it would be at least another five years before the textile factory would be able to produce lace and cloth.

***

Halfway between Saint-Quentin and Paris, they also passed by
the Compiègne forest. When, on November 11, 1918, the armistice treaty was signed there in a train car, André had been
standing in the square in the middle of Brussels, unable to com-
prehend what he saw: German soldiers tearing off their epaulettes
and medals from their uniform jackets and exchanging them for
red roses or a red insignia. French workers fraternized with their

Belgian counterparts, waving the French flag, the red Communist flag, and the Belgian flag, singing "La Marseillaise," and calling for a republic of workers and soldiers. "Down with capitalism!" "Fire the bosses!" the shouts rang. That this miserable war had been forced on them by the aristocrats and the capitalists was as clear to them as the morning sun. Now, finally, they could stand in solidarity and join themselves across national boundaries with others who belonged to the same economic class as they did. How stupid that they had been shooting each other!

The mood in the square had created a powerful yearning that seized André. To stand up as one among the many in such a crowd and wave a flag—what a powerful feeling that must be! As the demonstration slowly shifted into a drunken binge, however, André's desire to participate rapidly dissipated. Once again, he stood at the edge, alienated and estranged.

Now here he was in Paris, an enormous, unknown city, in a new school (the famous Lycée Buffon), with new classmates who divided themselves into refugees and "true" Parisians. But, finally, he also found a place in which he felt at home: the Fédé, a group of Protestant students who gathered in the Parisian art and science district on the left bank of the Seine River.[1] In Saint-Quentin, André would have loved to participate in a YMCA group, but his father had forbidden it. Such an uncivilized crowd was not suitable for a Trocmé. The confusion of war had not eliminated these social prejudices, but it had shaken them. Now, in his new home in Paris, André was even allowed to accompany the Fédé on a camping trip to the Ile d'Oléron, an island off the Atlantic coast. Here André experienced the pinnacle of independence. Young men lay about on the beach, sunning themselves without their shirts! Women were nowhere nearby, of course—the camp was

---

1 The Fédé (short for Fédération protestante de France), which was formed in 1905, united various Protestant Christian groups in France.

not mixed gender—but for André, who could scarcely imagine going a single day without his tie, it was an experience about which he enthused decades later. "For the first time in my life I did things simply because they were fun to do!"

The group also sang, prayed, and studied the Bible. This adventuresome mix of campfires, devotional times, and easy conversation was a completely new world for André. Here in this circle of Fédé friends, a desire that had been growing within him for two years took hold with new clarity: André wanted to study theology and become a Protestant pastor.

Nevertheless, it was not easy to tell his father of his vocational plans. His father's expectations for his children were so clear and so strict that André wasn't sure a career in the ministry would please him. He finally worked up the nerve to tell his father. "Papá," he said, using the formal form of address, "I would like to become a pastor."

"Good," said his father. "That pleases me. That is a very noble goal. In that case, you need to work on enunciating your words more clearly."

It was true: André often mumbled, sometimes even stuttered, when he spoke to his father. The same thing happened in other tense situations, such as when he had to give an impromptu speech in school. Even though he was otherwise a brilliant student, André often left an unfavorable impression in public.

"If your mother were here now," his father continued, "she would be happy. When you were born, we both committed you to God and hoped that you would one day become a pastor. I never told you that before, because I did not want to influence any of my children unduly. But if you have arrived at this decision yourself . . . then I am very happy. It's a good thing."

Paul Trocmé then told his son about the Easter morning when André was born and had received the middle name Pascal. "When you were finally born, your mother asked me to open the window as wide as possible so that the Easter morning sun and the tolling of the bells from the cathedral could fill the whole room."

The cathedral bells were gone, melted into cannons by the German soldiers. But the promise of that Easter morning seemed to have borne good fruit.

In the fall of 1919, André began his theology studies. And since he had always felt underchallenged as a student, he was determined to avoid this unpleasant feeling right from the start. So he matriculated in the graduate school of religious studies at the venerable Sorbonne. Any thought of boredom was completely forgotten, especially since alongside his studies he also pursued a second university entrance exam in other subjects—philosophy, natural history, German, and English. And all the while he continued his involvement with the Fédé, as well as with another Christian student club.

***

At the same time, something else emerged that made André truly happy. Robert, his favorite brother, who was fourteen years older than André, married a young woman from an upper-class Protestant family and moved to Paris. From that moment on, Robert made it his task to open the eyes of his younger brother to the treasures of the city.

Until then, André had walked through the city—what some Christians called the "whore of Babylon"—with his eyes lowered to the ground. Until then, the church and the university had been his worlds, and he had believed nothing else existed other than temptations and deceit, which a young man would do well to avoid. Now, however, Robert showed him that Paris was more than just books, on the one hand, and tawdry amusements, on the other. It also, for example, contained an enormous world of art. Together they visited the Louvre, where André was overcome by an epiphany while standing before the paintings of Giotto and Fra Angelico, the great Italian painters of the fourteenth century. There was more to the world than the austere, pictureless Protestant world, in which everything was either black or white, good or bad. Alongside all this there also existed an illuminated world with bewilderingly powerful, astonishingly beautiful works of art. A whole cosmos of art. And until this day he'd had no inkling of it!

André spent two exciting years with Robert in Paris. "Robert made it clear that we—Pierre and I—were completely uneducated in the ways of literature, music, and art," André wrote. So Robert did something unimaginable for the lifestyle of the Trocmés: he established an account from which his two younger brothers could draw money that would fund cultural activities.

> "Buy the books that you simply want to read," he told us. "No textbooks; only novels. Go to concerts; go to the theater. And be sure to tell me when the account is empty and I will refill it directly."
>
> It was unimaginable. In the shortest possible time, Robert taught us things about which we had no concept whatsoever: 1. There are things in life outside of absolute duties that also have value. 2. One can read for no other reason than pleasure. 3. If something is fun, you can learn without much effort. 4. There is such a thing as beauty.
>
> I was a young man who was trapped between a puritanical upbringing and all the accompanying struggles of an adolescent, on the one hand, and a thirst for absolutes, my religious ardor, and my rather Germanic-Romantic streak, on the other. Robert showed me what beauty was—physical and moral. He prepared the way which would one day lead me to Magda, my original, authentic, and creative Florentine.

***

In 1921, André interrupted his studies to begin a period of compulsory military service. Years had passed since his conversations with Kindler, the German soldier who had developed conscientious objections to war. The possibility of conscientious objection to military service did not exist, and André simply decided to make the best out of the situation. Nevertheless, he surprised himself. He had never imagined that the military could impress him so much. What a huge influence a troop commander had! And what dedication a commander had for his people!

> In Morocco, where I was stationed for six months, the officer's life seemed so attractive that in certain moments—actually, at precisely the same moments that I had doubts about my Christian faith—I considered the possibility of letting go of the idea of becoming a pastor and staying in the military. Suddenly, I faced the question of "all or nothing." Either I would give everything to the collective to which I belonged: my fatherland. Not just my life but also my soul and my spirit. I would obey in every instance; my conscience would be the conscience of an officer. I would do what I was ordered in times of peace as well as in times of war. That meant that I would renounce my belief in Jesus Christ, the prince of peace, the Son of God, the nonviolent one who allowed himself to be crucified because he refused to yield his obedience to the powerful of his time. Or I would give everything to Jesus Christ—my body, my soul, my spirit—obeying his commands without discussion, including the command that "Thou shalt not kill" and forgiveness of all that was owed to me.
>
> I chose the second path, although not because of my merit. My calling was simply overwhelmingly powerful.

This decision was the most important decision in André's life. Without it he would have never become a man whose biography must be written.

André rejected any military duties involving weapons. For this he was demoted to the "compagnie disciplinaire"—the disciplinary unit. Since it was not yet possible to even dream about an option of civil alternative service, André was happy to learn that he was able to transfer into the geographical service in Morocco, where he was given assignments that were boring but not a punishment. As an astronomer's assistant, he helped with the "measurements of the heavens," where he endured cold nights while entering data. It truly could have been worse.

Barely two years after his first day as a soldier, André returned to Paris and resumed his studies. Certain memories from his time in the military persisted, however, and haunted him. They related only indirectly to his own military service and focused more on the role of the French as a colonial power in Morocco. He did not want to keep these thoughts to himself, so during the winter semester he published an article in the *Bulletin des isolés*, a periodical by and for theology students.

There are things about which I only slowly have become aware that fill me with horror: the brutal treatment of the Arabs, who are whipped to death, kicked in the stomach and face with boots, and their hands hacked off. Eyewitnesses have described to me these things as if they were completely normal and absolutely legitimate. What a monstrous burden of guilt the French are heaping upon themselves! And in the midst of this comes the alcohol, which in the past four or five years has flooded a population that is already suffering from syphilis. Thanks to the influence of French industrial and trade concerns, the altruistic Moroccans have become stingy. Christian civilization seems to me to be nothing other than an enormous hullabaloo, a single-minded pursuit of money. What kind of counter role could the Europeans have played if, instead of a love for wealth, they would have brought health—and Christ?

In two years of life far from his books, André had come to know a side of being French that he could no longer justify with patriotic sentiments. And since he had superb grades, he saw an opportunity to escape the country for a time by applying for a foreign scholarship. His first preference was archeological studies in the Near East. His second choice was a year in Edinburgh, England, to study with famous professors. The third choice, which he regarded only as an emergency option, was a year at Union Theological Seminary in New York. André had no inkling, of course, that only a few years later the highly talented Dietrich Bonhoeffer would also choose this location.

The first two scholarships went to other applicants. So André was forced to decide whether to accept the third option. On the one hand, he did not anticipate much from a country of lumberjacks and trappers, the images that came first to mind when he thought about America. One the other hand, it was precisely his desire to escape the narrow, snobbish circles of his family and the intellectual, Franco-centric world in which he had been moving that had sparked the idea of foreign travel in the first place. New York would be far enough away, and it would provide a good contrast.

The decision became clear when André's father entered the picture. Paul Trocmé had moved back to Saint-Quentin and was already envisioning his very promising son as a pastor in the neighboring village. He was opposed to André spending time abroad, in any case; what could such a year possibly do for an aspiring French pastor? But he was especially opposed to New York.

André sensed that it was now up to him to set the course for his future. He accepted the scholarship and, in September 1925, left his home and his fatherland aboard a transatlantic steamer.

PART III

9

Walking the Emmaus Road

New York, 1926

He was tall, and he took such large strides with his long legs that in only a few steps he was once again walking ahead of her instead of alongside her. And yet it was the first stroll that he had ever taken with a woman, and he wanted nothing more than to be close to her.

Magda was the one. There was no longer any whisper of a doubt. Nothing but jubilation. Forty years later, André confirmed in writing what he had experienced on that evening: "She belonged to me and I to her!"

They walked along Amsterdam Avenue in the northwestern part of Manhattan. Both were still feeling new and strange in this enormous city, although they had now lived in New York for months—he as a theology student and she as an aspiring social worker. The academic year would soon be finished, but it was only a few days earlier, during a group excursion, that they had exchanged their first words.

The group had traveled by train to Washington, D.C., to visit all the requisite sites: the National Cathedral, Arlington National Cemetery, Mount Vernon. They had seen all the important tourist attractions and listened to long explanations. But he had perceived all of that as only background noise. In truth, he had seen only *her*—one moment fascinated and the next moment shocked. She was beautiful, but she smoked, and he could not stand women who smoked. She was Italian and spoke English and French with a sharp Italian accent. She had lively, intelligent eyes. But she seemed to be deeply unsettled, always inwardly restless.

His observations had stirred him so much that he returned to New York ahead of schedule and without informing his traveling companions. During a sleepless night, André asked the same questions over and over: Did this woman fit with the life he wanted to lead? Can one live like Gandhi and be married at the same time? Was it even possible to devote oneself to a life of poverty and have a family? And what about the world tour that was to follow the year in New York, and the visit to Tagore, the famous poet and activist, in India? Would he need to renounce all that? And what about the day he would become a Reformed pastor in France? Magda made many strong criticisms of the church. Could she live the classic life of a pastor's wife? It was hard to imagine.

But now, here on Amsterdam Avenue, André suddenly had the feeling of being on the Emmaus road, as he wrote later. There was an overwhelming certainty that pushed aside every possible doubt: I've found what I've always been seeking!

***

On the night of that walk, André had gone to the International House where Magda lived. Despite his awkward and sudden departure a few days earlier, he had arranged a gathering with the "Washington friends" for an evening meal. When he got to the foyer of the International House, he learned that everyone else had begged off. The Swiss fellow was injured, the Russian student was sick, and even Magda's friend, who had laughed so loudly on the train to Washington and smoked without any inhibition—even she had other plans. So it was only the two of them standing in the foyer: Magda and André.

"Yes, well, mademoiselle . . ." he said from above, looking more at the part in her black hair than at her face. A sudden desire to flee overcame him. "Maybe another time," he was about to say.

But she spoke first. "Then let's visit Skitzky," she said, already walking out the door. Skitzky was the sick Russian student.

So they visited the patient. More precisely, Magda expressed sympathy for the patient's condition, chatted, laughed, and held forth. Just as in Washington, she spoke about God and the world, about all sorts of grand things, about developments in Europe and America, and about the life she was living and the life she hoped to live. André also said a few words, but above all he watched Magda. Then, suddenly, they were standing again on the street and walking parallel to the Hudson River in the direction of the International House.

"As soon as we were together, I was overwhelmed with a sense of intimacy, one could almost say of identity," André wrote later. "But then I was suddenly filled with panic. If I continue like this, I told myself, I'm going to declare my love to her. I won't be able to restrain myself. And I'm not ready for that. I haven't thought about this fully enough. I don't want to tie myself down."

André stopped walking. "I'm very sorry, mademoiselle," he said softly, "but I think it would be better if I never saw you again.

Please excuse me." He did not even pause long enough to shake her hand. Several long strides, and he vanished.

"I didn't understand a single word of his mumbling in French," Magda admitted later.

André had not even reached his student apartment when he was overcome with a feeling of inner turmoil and despair. He stormed into his room, sat down, and tried to compose a clear mind, to concentrate, to pray. The face of his father flashed before him. How could he ever explain to him that he wanted to marry this Italian Protestant woman who was by no means a picture of perfection? He thought of the stories that were told around the table at home—stories of pastors who had ruined their careers by choosing the wrong spouse. But this Italian woman, Magda— wasn't she incredibly idealistic, obliging, and generous?

"And I left her alone to walk in the dark to the International House!" The thought pierced him.

André jumped up and ran in the direction of the Hudson. Of course there was no trace of Magda. She had surely returned home long ago. In the large hall of the International House, the lights were on. There was dancing on Friday nights.

"I want to see Miss Grilli," he said to the woman who sat beside the elevator to ensure that no man reached the floor of the women's sleeping quarters.

"It's impossible, sir," said a woman behind him. "You know the rules."

He turned and found himself facing Elizabeth, the most sought-after student in the house. She scrutinized him sternly.

"So you're the one," she said sharply.

"Yes. But where is Miss Grilli? Has she returned?"

"Of course she returned," Elizabeth said. "But beside herself with tears. What did you do to her?"

"Could you perhaps ask her to come down?"

Before long, Magda stood before him.

"Were you also thinking about me?" André asked carefully.

She nodded silently.

"I still need to think about it," he said. "I would like very much to see you again in a few days."

He set a deadline of two days hence. By Sunday evening he hoped to have restored order to his mind and heart. He locked himself in his room and took out a blank piece of white paper, divided it in half with a line, wrote "Pro" and "Con" at the top, tried in vain to pray, then gave up and filled in the pro column from top to bottom.

***

On Sunday, April 18, 1926, right after the worship service, he ran up the outside stairs to the International House.

"What's up, Troc? You look pleased with yourself," a student called out to him.

"Why not?" he answered, smiling. "I'm just about to become engaged."

It never for a moment occurred to him that the woman whom he had chosen could have said anything other than yes.

Mademoiselle Grilli di Cortona was expecting him. Her fashionable dress seemed to fit tighter than usual. She pulled on a camelhair coat and then a bowler hat. Her hands trembled a bit; the large needle that was supposed to secure her braid got stuck in the hat. She smiled and shrugged her shoulders. She was ready.

Silently the two left the apartments together. Silently they walked down 125th Street. Silently they sat beside each other on the bench of the ferry and watched as the New Jersey coastline drew closer. There on the rocks, where skyscrapers now look out over the Hudson River, the pair found a quiet little spot between the tall grass and the dense bushes.

"Would you be my wife?" André asked. "I am going to become a Protestant pastor, and I would like to live a life of poverty. I am a conscientious objector to war, and that could lead to prison and all sorts of other difficulties."

It was only the third time that they had been together.

Magda did not say yes, but she also did not say no. She began with a list of all the things that spoke against their relationship. It was a long list. She began by recounting difficult childhood experiences from her past and ended with a reference to her shaky health and an undiagnosed fever that haunted her every evening.

When she was finished with her list, she was quiet for a moment. Then she said, "Nevertheless, if you want to stand by your offer, then we will see what happens."

"I thought she was strong," André thought. "But she is weak. I wanted to lean on her for support, but it seems as if she will be the one leaning on me. Will I ever have enough strength for two people?"

But there she sat—honest, earnest, and weak. The woman he loved.

"Et voilà," Magda wrote in her memoirs. "From this day forward we regarded ourselves as engaged."

***

The news made the rounds, and friends at Union Theological Seminary, where André was studying, celebrated enthusiastically. But for the following months, André communicated nothing to his family. He waited so long to tell them that Magda began to think he was going to back out of the commitment. But then André sat himself down and wrote his father a letter with three points: one, he was engaged; two, he intended to marry in the United States; and three, the couple was planning to travel back to France, although the trip would take them first to India; since they did not have enough money to finance the world tour, he planned to find work on the ship.

The response was prompt: there was no shortage of globe-trotters in France, but France did have a shortage of pastors ready to fulfill their calling and their duties.

10

Serve the Rich or the Poor?

New York, 1926

So now they were engaged: Magda, an impassioned Italian aristocrat, daughter and granddaughter of a Russian and Italian military family, who was studying social work in the city of her dreams. And André, earnest offspring of a French industrial and German pastoral dynasty, who was studying theology in a city that had been his third choice.

What did the engaged couple do? They spent as much time as possible with each other. They tried to get to know each other better. They busied themselves with preparations for the wedding and the marriage ahead.

There wasn't any topic that didn't trigger some sort of worry for Magda and André. "The first weeks of our engagement were not very happy," André summarized in his notes. Both had taken on jobs in addition to their studies—jobs that almost occupied more of their energy than their studies themselves and, even

worse, monopolized their time nearly every weekend. "My fiancée was completely overworked," wrote André.

> But still she [was] . . . always going back to her work. She worked
> like a fiend. Alongside her classes at the New York School of
> Social Work and a stressful practicum, she loaded herself down
> with French and Italian tutoring that kept her busy until ten in
> the evenings. And then she still didn't go to bed. This hectic pace
> worried me. When we did find time to meet it was always late in
> the day. We sat together in the parlor of the International House,
> a room with marvelous tapestries depicting the conquest of the
> Americas. . . . She was often nervous, always thinking about lots
> of little things that still needed to be done, while I wanted to talk
> about love and philosophy.

The time that Magda and André spent together was not
only extremely limited but also often overcast with dark clouds.
Opportunities to get to know each other better were limited not
only because Magda was bustling about; André's overly full plan
of study was also an issue. Although André had a scholarship, life
in New York City was not cheap, and his father was not the sort
of man to give his son spending money for "extras." By tradition,
the Trocmés lived within their means. Moreover, to grant André
his own bank account could make possible a lifestyle that would
be regarded as immoral. So when André arrived in New York in
September 1925, for example, he was wearing a raincoat he had
found in a closet for needy students at the theology department
in Paris.

***

All of this changed in October, when a secretary at the seminary
called André to the phone. Someone was trying to reach him.

"My name is John D. Rockefeller Jr., Fifty-Fourth Street," said the man, "and I need a French tutor for my son. I was very pleased with your fellow students whom I've hired in the last years—perhaps you knew Westphal, Couve, and Theis? If you are interested, then set up an appointment with Mrs. Rockefeller."

"Yes . . . yes . . . I'll be in touch," was all André could say. He set the heavy telephone in the cradle. That was the end of the conversation.

Rockefeller? *The* Rockefeller? Had he just spoken with the richest man in the world? No, that couldn't be. The man was as old as the hills and surely did not have any children who needed tutoring in French. So it must have been the son. Still, it was unbelievable. Someone must have recommended him.

"Mr. Rockefeller is a great benefactor of our organization," the secretary said, pulling André out of his stupor. "Without him, we would not have the International House. It's very important for him that we expose foreign students to a little bit of democracy if they happen to be in the States."

And now André had a chance to expose the Rockefeller children to a bit of French. André shook his head. Teaching the heirs of vast oil fields—children of a family that had not suffered during the war, but rather saw its fortunes increase thanks to the catastrophe in Europe? Wars, after all, consume so much oil. And he, of all people, was to be their teacher.

The next day André stood at the door of the Rockefeller residence. The house at 10 West Fifty-Fourth Street did not call attention to itself. Five floors with large windows, each covered with a cage-like structure of iron bars—the kingdom of the six Rockefeller children. Through a collusion between the Standard Oil Company and the railroad lines, John D. Rockefeller Sr. had made himself so unpopular that he was forced to live in semi-isolation. As a result, his son, John D. Rockefeller Jr., was determined to do the opposite. He lived in the middle of the city and interacted with people every day. By the time that André appeared at his door, he had already contributed $400 million to worthy causes. In so doing, the generous son had clearly distinguished himself from his miserly father.

André did not stand alone at the door, nor did he press the doorbell himself. An armed man dressed in civilian clothes who had been walking up and down in front of the house accompanied him to the door and rang the bell for him.

And then André found himself sitting in the parlor across from John D. Rockefeller Jr., drinking tea and eating scones. "Fortunately, I wasn't alone," he wrote later. "A large, red-headed, very self-confident American immediately introduced himself to me as the English teacher. Thanks to his presence I didn't drop my cup, spoon, and sugar to the floor out of sheer excitement."

Abby Rockefeller soon joined them and informed the young French teacher of his duties—that was, if he was willing to take the job and if they were satisfied with him as a teacher. André was to be responsible for only the two youngest boys, Winthrop and David. Every afternoon around four o'clock they would need to be picked up at their school on the north end of Central Park and accompanied home on the bus. Then André was to drink an afternoon tea with them and oversee their homework. If he wished, he could stay for dinner afterward. On weekends he was expected to be present from Friday afternoon to Saturday evening at the family's country home some thirty miles north of the city on the banks of the Hudson River. Sundays were free.

It was three days after the Rockefellers hired him that André discovered just how much he was going to earn for this job: $175 a month! He promptly opened a savings account. Eight months multiplied by $175 would add up to $1,400 in savings! Ever since the beginning of his studies in Paris, André had dreamed of taking a trip around the world and meeting Gandhi and Tagore. Maybe a trip to India would provide him with answers to the many questions that preoccupied him—questions about violence and nonresistance, about power and the strength of those who appeared to be powerless. Now, suddenly this dream was not merely a foolish illusion but a realistic possibility. What a crazy world: he would now be working for the richest of the rich in order to make possible a visit to the Indian guru of poverty and simplicity.

The tasks of accompanying and instructing the Rockefeller sons proved to be straightforward. André could hardly believe how little homework American students had to complete in comparison to the French—although the children, of course, regarded it as far too much. He spoke both French and English to "Winnie" and David, and along the way deepened his own understanding of American slang, which he never encountered in his theological studies.

On the weekends, André also got to know the other Rockefeller children. The family openly expressed the hope that Nelson, the third child, would one day become president of the United States (he pursued this several times in vain, though he did serve late in his life as vice president under Gerald Ford); the family also had clear expectations about the roles the other children were to play in life. At the same time, Mr. and Mrs. Rockefeller tried, as much as possible, to hide from the children the full extent of the family fortune. This was no easy task when a servant stood day and night behind concealed doors, who would instantly appear at the gentle ring of a bell to ask, "Your wish?" Even André could not refrain from availing himself at least once.

"The parents of the Gautama Buddha tried to hide their child from the realities of sickness, aging, and death. Mr. and Mrs. Rockefeller tried to give their children a fixed amount of spending money from which they needed to buy their books and school supplies," André wrote. "Nonetheless, they had become smug already as children and were bored with everything." The children knew that they would never have to work a day in their lives, and that anything that might be "lacking" was only for pedagogical reasons and would not be denied them in the long run.

The Rockefellers treated their employees with gracious courtesy, although it remained obvious that they lived in two different worlds. "To say it even more clearly: we didn't really exist for our students," André wrote. And just who needed to learn from whom was clear. Sometimes André managed to laugh about it; sometimes not.

"Young man, I'm going to do something for you!" the elder Rockefeller, John Sr., said one day when André had the dubious pleasure of being a guest in his palatial residence. "I'm going to give you a dime. Promise me that you will invest this money as soon as you return to your country! That's exactly how I started, and how I became rich."

André earnestly promised to so do and put the coin in his pocket. Then he received a dime for his father, which he also pocketed.

"Do you have siblings?" asked the eighty-seven-year-old.

"Yes, seven," answered André.

"That's too many. That will drive me to bankruptcy!" And so things were left at twenty cents.

"More gasoline and higher prices—that's what we need" were the parting words that John D. Rockefeller Sr. left with his guest. Those words remained with André for a long time. Many years later he noted in his memoirs: "I have always marveled at people—without understanding them—who believe that they have the solution to every problem in the world simply because they themselves, through luck or hard work, have achieved success." The gently ironic tone in his words is unmistakable.

***

André lived between two worlds. When he returned to the city by train from the Rockefeller country home on Saturday evenings, he would meet with a group of students led by Bill Simpson, a thirtysomething friend who had committed himself to a celibate, solitary life among working-class people in one of the poorest neighborhoods of New York City. Simpson wanted to develop a Christian form of Gandhism—an initiative that fascinated André and which he would have loved to join on the spot.

Back at the Rockefeller home, André was informed that the family would be very pleased if he would stay for another year. Beyond his tasks as a tutor, they said, he might be given an opportunity to support John Rockefeller Jr. in his global philanthropic work. But the theology school had also offered André the possibility of extending his studies for another year in order to start a doctoral program, and the Rockefeller family would be happy to underwrite the costs.

As if the decision between these two paths were not difficult enough, André also received many letters from his father about the great need for Protestant pastors in the northern part of France. After the upheaval of 1918, pastors were especially focused on the material and spiritual needs of the working class.

Each of these opportunities had its own appeal. Every cause was important. For André, each task seemed like exactly the right direction. Was he called now to poverty? Or to serve the rich in order to earn money for the poor? And then there was his engagement. Magda. What was her calling? Or was a woman automatically called to do the things her husband was called to do?

One day even Abby Rockefeller noticed that Magda was overworked, unsettled, and very underweight. The engaged couple had been invited to celebrate the eleventh birthday of one of the children. The lady of the house soon had an idea. "I'll give the two of you a wedding present right now, in advance," Mrs. Rockefeller said. "Take a break from your studies, Miss Grilli—assuming, that is, that you even want to continue them, since it's actually not necessary anymore—and spend several weeks in Clifton Springs. Up north, close to Canada, the climate is pleasant and there are the famous sulfur springs. If you would spend a little time in a sanatorium there, you will be able to take on your duties as a housewife in the very best condition!"

Magda accepted the gift, and the little time she and André had together shrank even further to a few hours every second Sunday afternoon. André would take the night train north from the Rockefeller country house, sit down beside Magda—who would first lie in her room and then rest outside on a chaise longue with wheels—and watch as the woman who was to become his wife regained her strength.

"If you think that I'm not healthy enough," said Magda one day, "and if you think I don't believe the right things, then say it, and we'll end the engagement!"

André was distraught. Not only was he unsure of the particular form of his calling, but now even his calling to marry Magda was in question. These things tossed and turned in his heart and mind on the return trip. Nothing was certain anymore. Everything was in doubt.

Soon thereafter, a conversation with a doctor helped André see things more clearly. "Miss Grilli is very nervous—that's true," the doctor said. "And there's nothing that we can do about the light fever that she gets every evening. The tonsillectomy did nothing to help this. But these are all physical problems, not psychological ones. I would advise you to marry. Of course, it will be your task to do everything you can to lighten the burden for your wife and not tire her. And she certainly will need to lie down and rest every afternoon for two or three hours."

A pastor to the working class? A disciple of Gandhi? A philanthropic world traveler representing the wealthy Rockefellers? Or simply a modest French pastor, whose most important task would be to tend to his wife?

Eventually, André resolved internally the question of the future. He wrote his father and announced that the wedding would take place that same summer. He later wrote, "Only in the course of time would I recognize the extraordinary love and endless commitment of which Magda was capable."

11

Wedding and Travels

Saint-Quentin, 1926–Florence, 1926

Magda's family had warned her against the marriage. ("Do you seriously want to be the wife of a Protestant pastor?") André's family warned him too. ("An Italian woman? Have you thought carefully about this?") How simple it would have been to forget all the naysayers in Europe and simply get married in the United States, preferably in the summer, in a modest ceremony beneath a tree at the beautiful, remote Clifton Springs and accompanied by a small circle of friends.

The couple had already convinced a retired Methodist bishop to help them go through with this plan when a letter arrived from Paul Trocmé in France. If his son was actually going to marry this Italian, he said, then please hold the ceremony at home, in France, rather than in some land far from family. Traditionally, that would mean the home of the bride's parents, but since Magda did not really have a home of her own, she should henceforth consider the Trocmé family as her family. Naturally, Monsieur Grilli di

Cortona, Magda's father, was warmly welcome to attend the wedding in Saint-Quentin.

André's fantasy of a trip to India after the wedding seemed, even to him, increasingly out of the question. "In fifteen or sixteen months you will have a family to feed," wrote André's father, "and hopefully you do not wish to impose the life of a gypsy on your poor wife. Do you really want to put her in a tiny room full of bedbugs and have your children living in some ghastly, unhealthy place?"

The letter could not have been more clear. Gone was the dream of a summer wedding under a big tree. But André's father was not the only voice opposing a summer wedding. Friends in Clifton Springs wanted Magda to stay there for several more weeks. Despite all the nourishment she was receiving, her weight was still not where it should be. And then the Rockefeller family asked André to accompany them on their summer vacation to the western United States.

"We felt a bit as if our wings had been clipped," wrote Magda. "But that was the price. Now I had a family. I had a place where I could get married; I was accepted. Later I realized that I was more than accepted—Paul Trocmé, the chief of the clan and the commander of a platoon of seven sons, received me with great warmth."

So in the fall of 1926, the young couple said goodbye to their American friends and boarded a ship in New York. The long passage finally gave the couple unlimited time for conversation, and André noticed with surprise and joy that Magda was eagerly looking forward to the encounter with his family. Until this point in her life she had never seen a "normal" family from the inside. Now she would become acquainted with a grand family, rich in tradition and governed by an old-fashioned patriarch, in which everything was well regulated and where everyone—from the oldest great-aunt to the youngest grandchild—knew his or her place and was united by a common faith.

Magda encountered the highly regulated nature of the Trocmé family on the evening of their arrival. After a year abroad, André had brought with him a fiancée known to the family only through letters. But at the evening meal, Magda and André sat alone at the large table in the middle of the spacious dining room. The family, as was its custom, had already eaten promptly at seven in the evening, before the two arrived. This was not out of a lack of interest or a deficiency in warmth. It was simply the way things were done.

Gradually, various members of the family gathered around the couple as they ate, and they seated themselves on chairs that were lined up along the walls. Their attention focused especially on Magda, and they expressed their assessments. Out loud. "She is much prettier than in the photos," claimed Francis, André's oldest brother. The others agreed. And then André's father offered the highest praise of all as he referenced the modest, dark dress that Magda had purchased especially for this first appearance. "That's just the way it should be," Paul Trocmé said. "She's wearing long sleeves, and she has long hair."

Evidently, speaking the truth was a particularly valued quality of the family's Protestant convictions. Magda would gradually become accustomed to it.

***

For nearly six weeks the young couple circulated under the watchful eyes of the family—along with those of a maid and a cook, who were both supposed "to keep an eye on" André and Magda. Confirming a date for their wedding became difficult. First they were missing the necessary papers from Italy; then they needed an officially approved translation. Despite numerous letters, telephone calls, admonishments, and long waits outside offices, it was the middle of November before the last stamp finally appeared in the right place.

The family records of the newly married couple say almost nothing about the actual wedding in Saint-Quentin. Because the courthouse had been destroyed in the war, all civil ceremonies had to take place in the town hall. Magda and André's marriage was to be the first in the newly opened civil registry, but the person in charge had forgotten the appointment. So he quickly donned his sash and married the couple in a half-finished room in the middle of a construction site. At the church celebration the next day, traces of the decorations from a funeral were still visible.

André's memoirs mention only the evening of their wedding day: "On the evening of our wedding we waited at the Gare de Lyon [a train station in Paris] for a train that would take us to Italy," he wrote. "We wanted to eat something, but not in a restaurant. That evening I learned just how much my young wife loved everything associated with picnics. I hate picnics. But finally, we sat on some steps and ate the ham sandwiches that we brought with us. The train compartment we had reserved was old and smelled of stale cigarette smoke. We couldn't sleep."

Nonetheless, both of them would happily and frequently recall the honeymoon for the rest of their lives. They traveled first from France to Switzerland. For Magda, French was the proper language of her childhood, and now it was the language that joined her to André. But she had never been in France itself. For his part, André had visited the Atlas Mountains and the Rocky Mountains, but he had never seen the Alps. Nor had he been to Italy. After several days in the Bernese Oberland in Switzerland, they traveled to Venice, the classic destination for newlyweds. Then to Trieste, Fiume Veneto, Ancona, and then to Assisi, which in those days was still untouched by tourists. The couple wanted to thoroughly enjoy the relaxing and fun part of their honeymoon before they faced the Grilli di Cortona family.

***

The closer they got to Florence, the more nervous Magda became. Florence proved itself to be gray and unwelcoming. After weeks of uninterrupted autumn sunshine, they reached the city in a downpour. Nothing had changed in the years of Magda's absence. The reception of Oscar, Magda's father, was reserved—he needed to be considerate of his wife, Marguerite. Oscar first invited the couple to supper in a restaurant without his wife; afterward they went for tea and a few cookies at the parental home. That encounter with Magda's stepmother lasted a half hour, and the atmosphere was frigid.

Magda came down with a severe cold, and in the days that followed, André viewed the art treasures of the city in the company of an old professor, whose insights he failed to fully appreciate in light of the fact that Magda was home in bed. Only later did the couple discover that Falkenberg, Magda's despairing and persistent suitor, had been following their trail and had spied on them from behind a column in the train station at the time of their arrival.

Once Magda recovered from her cold, a series of invitations followed. Each evening they dined with a different family from Florentine high society. The hosts would greet André with a few sentences in French, and then the conversation would shift to Italian. The atmosphere was usually loud, lively, and jocular, with Magda in the middle of it, spirited and completely in her element. "In Florence I came to understand that I had married an Italian," was André's laconic summary of those days.

From another perspective, however, Magda was far less Italian than André had assumed before the trip. When Magda occasionally explained to him how things functioned in the Grilli family, André had always assumed that she was exaggerating. The terrible jealousy, the resentment—all of this was surely a bit overstated. He, as a calm, rational Frenchman, thought he would likely find all of this to be far less dramatic. André was wrong. He was now forced to acknowledge that Magda had not been exaggerating in the slightest. Marguerite, her stepmother, was still sick with jealousy, even after many years of marriage to Oscar. And she was particularly jealous of Magda, who had grown up long ago and no longer lived in Florence. Even Magda and André's marriage did not change the feelings that haunted Magda's stepmother. For the entirety of her life, Marguerite would forbid her children—Magda's half siblings—to visit the young Trocmé couple or even to write to them. Even Oscar, her husband, had to write and send letters to his daughter in secret.

"Magda truly was alone in life," André wrote. "And so my wife, probably more than other wife, still looks back on her childhood years with regret. Her life and my life became as one. She married not only a man but also his job and his calling. And she did so with remarkable passion and remarkable clear-sightedness. Not once was she tempted to look backward. And I, who had never been focused on the past, whose eyes were always directed to the future—I, with my special sense for the present, had a clear ally."

The year 1927 had begun. In northern France, duty called.

Young Family
in Coal Country

Maubeuge, 1927–Sin-le-Noble, 1933

M aubeuge is one of the ugliest cities in France." With this
sentence, André began his recollections of his first pastoral assignment. If one comes from New York via Florence and
settles in Maubeuge—a coal-mining backwater in the French-
Belgium border region—then one can only experience it as a kind
of imposition.

> A row of small cities extending for some 25 kilometers
> [fifteen miles] along the muddy water of the Sambre. Amid the
> houses of blackened bricks, the reddish soot of the ironworks
> congeals like a fatty crust on roofs, walls, and streets, forcing
> its way even into the houses themselves. Since they had no
> cars, the inhabitants, whose lives depended on heavy industry
> (smelting furnaces, rolling mills, wire-drawing mills, foundries,
> and glassworks) could never escape to somewhere green. So they
> plodded through life with a numbness that is hard to imagine.

It was not that they were so poor—that was the first thing that amazed us. After all, it's impossible to persuade people to take up work that is going to ruin their health within twenty years if you don't lure them with good wages. But the people knew nothing of life apart from their extremely demanding labor and the corner bar, in which they drank themselves into unconsciousness.

The young couple's dreary impression of the city was heightened by André's first encounter with his supervisor, Paul Perret, the head pastor serving in the region. Swiss by birth, Perret was a busy, impatient person who drove himself and others to the very edge in advancing the cause of the Lord. If there was one thing that he could not understand, it was the carefree way in which the young couple had spent an entire month on their honeymoon, cruising through the world while the needs of the industrial workers in Maubeuge were crying out to the heavens. Thus, André's first moments in his professional career began with a proper scolding. Then it was time to get to work—which, as André soon noted, had far less to do with classic congregational tasks than with social work, with a particular focus on alcoholics.

The first shared apartment that Magda and André occupied had a promising-sounding address: 1 rue de l'Hermitage, Sous-le-Bois (1 Hermit Street, Below the Small Woods). In reality, however, Sous-le-Bois was a miserably dirty suburb of Maubeuge. If there had ever been a small woods or a hermitage there, they were no longer to be found.

Their home at 1 rue de l'Hermitage had formerly been a guesthouse. The entrance led into the largest room, formerly a reception area, now divided by a wall to create a kind of pastor's study. The front part of the room served as an entry and cloakroom; the other, as André's workroom. The floor consisted of wooden planks laid directly on top of a compacted dirt floor—fortunately, there was no cellar into which one might have fallen. Walking across the boards, which were always sliding to and fro, you entered a small kitchen that connected to a dining room, which also served as the living room. At the top of a steep stairway were two small rooms on the upper floor, and then an even steeper stairway led to a tiny garret under the roof. In the small garden plot extending out from the kitchen stood a shack—an outhouse so frugally built that André with his long legs could barely close the door while seated. Since there were no lights and since the wind or rain often extinguished candles on the journey to the outhouse, André purchased a storm lantern.

The house was damp and did not have running water. Water for drinking, cooking, and washing had to be fetched from a pump in the garden. A drain from the ceramic sink in the kitchen flowed into a gutter alongside the street.

Located on the other side of the garden was the dance hall of the former guesthouse. Its function, in contrast to the main house, had not changed. It opened for dancing every Saturday evening, and the loud music resounded throughout the parsonage. André, who usually worked on his Sunday sermon on Saturday evenings, found that the noise grated on his every last nerve. Magda was more offended by the smell of cooking oil that filled the house on Saturday evenings. Whenever there was dancing, a french fry vendor set up his wagon directly in front of the parsonage.

Magda and André's neighbors were quite different from the mostly French residents in the center of Maubeuge. Nearly all their neighbors were from Poland or Italy. The goal of their sojourn in France was clear: to stay in this ghastly place for as short a time as possible before returning to their homeland. Some of them lived in the neighborhood for only a week, others for several months. So there was a steady stream of people moving in and out of the little black cottages. The shopkeepers along the long street leading to the steelworks were frequently left with

unpaid bills, since the workers who bought items on credit sub-
sequently returned to their home countries without settling their
accounts. This, of course, brought the store owners into further
economic hardship.

"A very interesting place, if someone wanted to pursue mis-
sions or social work," wrote Magda, somewhat dispassionately, in
her diary. She had plunged straightaway into the work at hand. It
was not worth the effort to invite the Poles or Italians to the small
Protestant church, which had some fifty members. The Polish and
Italian migrants were, without exception, Catholic, and would
never set foot in the place. But Magda found a neutral meeting space and offered classes for those women who, with their
husbands, were staying in France a bit longer than the others.
The theme was not doctrine or ethics or language or literature.
Instead, Magda explained the basic principles of hygiene, nutri-
tion, and baby care, mostly in Italian. During her practicum in
New York, her work had focused on places in crisis, and especially
among Italian immigrants. Magda herself had grown up with a
nanny and a cook, so when it came to groceries, she didn't even
know the names of all the vegetables. But when it came to her
classes with the women, her focus was not on culinary delicacies
but on more elemental things: how a person could avoid illnesses
and accidents and provide children with a healthy environment—
even if the father was an alcoholic who drank up all the income.

André, meanwhile, invested a portion of the savings that remained from his Rockefeller tutoring job in the installation of
water pipes to run from the garden to the kitchen of the parsonage. Magda was pregnant, and André couldn't bear the idea of her
standing in the garden in all kinds of weather and wrestling with
the heavy pump. That small reserve fund made their life somewhat easier. The trip to India, for which the money had originally been intended, was probably never going to happen. André's

income was less than modest. Unlike Germany, France had never instituted a church tax. Whoever worked for the church lived on donations. In those days the donations came not only in the form of money but also as gifts of clothes or food or other items from wealthier congregations in places like Paris. In addition, church administrators actively intended pastors who lived in places like Maubeuge to be poor. As much as possible there should be no gap between the pastor's lifestyle and that of the congregation.

But a gap existed nonetheless. André and Magda repeatedly tried to invite people from the congregation for meals. But the people they invited consistently turned them down. If they did come, they would say that they had already eaten. "They were afraid to eat with us," wrote Magda. "We did not belong to their milieu, and they didn't know how they were supposed to act with us. I was a foreigner, and André gave the impression of being a bit dignified and strict. . . . They simply did not know us well enough."

***

The Trocmés' first child, a girl, was born in the summer of 1927. They named her Nelly—short for Helena, after Magda's deceased mother.

Occasionally, when Magda and André were together during a quiet moment, they would ask themselves why André's father and the church administration—of which Paul Trocmé was a part—had made this pastoral assignment in Maubeuge such an urgent priority. The answer could not have been in the work itself. Nothing here was particularly well suited to André's gifts or interests.

Over the course of the summer, some thoughts occurred to them. First, they learned that André's predecessor in Sous-le-Bois had left after a bitter quarrel with his boss. Only those far from the scene—in New York, for example—would not have heard about the controversy, which had echoed throughout the Reformed Church. Furthermore, André had a particular quality that disqualified him for a position in the "better" congregations: he was a pacifist. To be sure, he had served in the military for a short period, but during that time he had refused to carry a weapon. Someone like that might be tolerated as a local pastor, but he could never hope for a true career in the church. Pastoral candidates were forbidden to be conscientious objectors. André clearly would have done better to stay in New York and pursue his doctorate.

But his father had worked so hard to bring his youngest son back home. Was Maubeuge a kind of trap into which they, with all their pious naiveté, had fallen? Every now and then, that disillusioning thought loomed before them. Yes, it was possible. But they did not want to see it that way. "Let's look at it as a step in my education," André said. "There are several things here that I can learn. . . . But this kind of teaching cannot last too long!"

***

A year later, in September 1928, the family moved to Sin-le-Noble, where André began his first solo pastorate. Once again, it was a place with a promising name. Noble had been a small medieval city, so named because it was directly accountable to the king. But the social conditions of the townspeople and parishioners were the same as in Maubeuge.

Magda and André decided that before André could preach to the people in Sin-le-Noble, they should first establish a soup kitchen. After all, there were many such initiatives in the United States. So André went to the mayor for permission. The mayor was not enthused by the zeal of the new pastor and his wife, and he imposed a condition: "You can do it only if you can persuade everyone to support the idea—from the far right [the Catholics] to the far left [the Communists]. Otherwise everyone is going to be against me in the next election."

The mayor's Catholic counterpart insisted that he had no say in such matters: "Everything that is needed here has already been provided by our nuns." From the local Communist Party, André received a decisive rejection: "In light of the imminent demise of the capitalist system, which we are already observing, the Communist Party cannot have any interest in keeping it alive through charitable actions," the chair of the party wrote. "The working class must recognize that this exploitative system, which victimizes them all, is already in a state of decay. Only then will they rise up against it—and that precisely is our goal."

So Magda and André had to give up the idea of a soup kitchen. Then, only a few days later, they received a surprise. Out on the street they heard the ringing of small bells. When they ran to the window, they saw a cart with a large sign: the Red Aid, a Communist social service agency, was seeking donations of potatoes and vegetables in support of the "exploited and starving working class."

"I never fully digested the hypocrisy of the Communists of Sin-le-Noble," André wrote later. "But they did teach me an important lesson: acts of solidarity can never serve the propagandists, but only those who are suffering. Otherwise they become weapons, and that is unfair."

By contrast, Magda and André had great success with another idea they borrowed from their time in America. Their idea helped to establish a tradition that the mayor of Sin-le-Noble later advertised as a unique quality of the city: namely, an "old-fashioned Christmas" that included a "real Father Christmas" who came on a sled. In contrast to Santa Claus in the United States, this French

André Trocmé (in back) with a group of young boys from his congregation in Sin-le-Noble. Private collection.

Father Christmas first made his rounds to collect donations, which he later distributed to the poor. And since none of the youth of the congregation wanted to make a fool of themselves during the initial event, André—who had always hated dress-up games as a child—reluctantly affixed a beard to his chin and pulled on a red coat. Since it was raining, he and Magda pulled a cart rather than a sled through the city. With his meager acting abilities, André tried to persuade people to make their donations. People initially thought that the two figures were complete lunatics, and taunted them. But someone finally recognized the pastor beneath the false beard and shouted to the others, "Shut your mouths! That's the boss from the temple!"[1] And with this first embarrassing appearance as Father Christmas, the little congregation and its pastor became known throughout the city.

---

1 In the Old Testament tradition, the Reformed Christians in France called the church building a "temple."

The Trocmés remained in Sin-le-Noble for six years. Three sons were born there: Jean-Pierre (1930), Jacques (1931), and Daniel (1933). Various au pairs, mostly from Germany, supported Magda during these years and also helped the family maintain a living connection to André's mother tongue.

The political landscape in Europe was changing—first in barely perceptible ways, and then much more noticeably. When Magda, for example, was offered a position as an Italian teacher, she initially regarded it as a good idea. But then she discovered that the curriculum was dictated by the Italian government. Benito Mussolini had been in control since 1922, and his influence was unmistakably reflected in the schoolbooks. With the help of this curriculum, teachers were supposed to openly support the principles of fascism. Magda refused—but she was still unable to prevent rumors that this left-leaning Italian exile was a fascist.

***

André slowly came to realize that the struggles unfolding on the world stage were intensifying. One day he sat in the office of the director of mines to ask for a favor. During the school holidays, there were no opportunities for the children of miners to spend their free time in a meaningful way. The older children were especially inclined to get caught up in all kinds of bad behavior. André knew exactly what these children needed. But the city had no rooms, not even a recreation field, where he could establish a summer vacation program. Close to the mining shafts, however, there was an unused piece of land.

"It can't be in our interests that a sect like yours takes interest in our children," said the director of the mines. "Why should we rent this piece of land to you of all people?"

Sect? André struggled to contain himself and then began to offer some polite clarifications.

"Okay, good," said the director after only a few sentences. "I have to acknowledge that your project has the goal of improving the moral character of the working class, and it is indeed clearly needed. So I'm ready to offer your organization the same use of our stadium and all the other sports facilities that we give to the Catholics."

What a surprising and abrupt change of attitude! And now the director was opening a drawer in his desk and offering André a bundle of cash. "We can also give you an annual subsidy," he said as he offered André two thousand francs. "This is for your project."

André couldn't believe what was happening. His congregation was so poor, and now, with a few sentences, he had raised two thousand francs for the children!

"There is one condition," the director said as he leaned back in his chair. "We are entering into troubled times and facing some social turmoil. This will not be easy. In your sermons, you can offer important counsel to your members. The Catholic priests have already promised to do so. Actually, it's in the miner's own best interest to cooperate with us. I'm quite sure that you will be able to make that understandable to them."

André was stunned. "Does that mean that I am to tell the workers they should oppose the unions?" he asked. "That they should even leave the union?"

André stood up. His face had become bright red. "I'm very sorry, sir, but my task is to preach the gospel. I can't comply with your request."

"Whatever you think," said the director. He took the money that André held out to him and returned it to the drawer, closing it carefully.

PART IV

13

Moving to the End
of the Earth

Sin-le-Noble, 1933–Le Chambon-sur-Lignon, 1934

There are no states or provinces in France. This means that virtually everything of importance—not only in politics but also in all matters related to school, culture, and church—is decided in Paris and orchestrated from Paris. This is very practical if you are moving your child from one school to another. But for a teacher, it means that you can be transferred to a new position anywhere in the entire country. Naturally, this is not always good news.

The Reformed Church of France, André's employer, operated in the same way. The Trocmés urgently wanted to leave northern France. From the time she was a baby, Nelly, the oldest child, had suffered from severe bronchitis, forcing her to spend periods of time in a pediatric hospital in Switzerland. The three boys were also sick almost constantly. Nearly every family in the congregation had at least one person suffering from tuberculosis; the first antibiotic treatments would not be available worldwide for another ten years. In addition, a second sickness raged that is nearly forgotten today: silicosis, also known as black lung disease. The illness, normally contracted only by those who had spent many days working underground, was triggered by breathing fine dust that contained quartz. In Sin-le-Noble, however, the air was so contaminated with mineral dust that the sickness could affect anyone, including children.

André heard that a pastoral position was about to become available in a working-class suburb south of Paris. He sent a written application, was invited to give a trial sermon, and interviewed with the church council. Everything was proceeding exactly according to church protocol, and both sides seemed to be very excited. André was open about his commitment to pacifism, but he promised not to use the pulpit to advocate for his position or to push it upon others. The church council was taken with the young, committed pastor and gave him a written intent to hire.

Everything was arranged, and the family began to make plans for the move. But suddenly the church administration in Paris intervened. A pacifist? So close to Paris? This would surely threaten the peace within church circles. The congregation would have to find a different pastor.

Incensed, André traveled to Paris and demanded a conversation with the church president.

"I did not summon you!" the president shouted angrily.

"I know," André responded, looking at him intently. "But I'm going to stay here until you hear me out."

For fifteen minutes André waited in the hallway. Then he was called into the conference room. Fifteen men had gathered there. André stood in front of them—no one invited him to take a seat. The men were obviously not intending for a small-town pastor with grand visions for transforming the world to steal their time.

"My dear Mr. Trocmé," said the church president. "I'm going to ask you only one question. Let's assume there is a war: Will you put on a uniform and defend the fatherland? Yes or no?" The president did not wait for an answer. "I know that you conscientious objectors have your pride. You don't want to get your hands dirty, so you prefer to turn to other people when it comes time to resist evil. We cannot give you the pastoral position that you have applied for. You may go."

Blindsided, André turned red and started for the door. But then the outrage that rose inside him found expression in a single sentence: "Gentlemen, it seems to me that in light of such a momentous decision it would be most appropriate for us to have a prayer together."

Fourteen mouths hung open; fourteen pairs of eyes glanced nervously around the room. Only the president kept his composure. "Brother Gounelle, would you please be so good as to offer a prayer."

Pastor Gounelle was the oldest person in the room. He prayed with a quavering voice, "Lord, bless your church and lead this young, misguided pastor back to the right path."

Several minutes later, the "young, misguided pastor" stood again outside the room. The veto of the church administration remained unshaken.

"No one said 'hello' or 'goodbye' to me," he wrote twenty years later. "I stood on the street in front of the door of the Reformed Church of France and could not have imagined that a second world war and the scandal of a collaboration with a victorious enemy would be necessary in order to plant a doubt in the hearts of these good patriots of 1914 that France was always right and would always remain right. How could a Christian doubt this or refuse to bear arms when the cause of France was always God's cause?"

***

So the search for a new position resumed. What other place could be suitable for a family with four small, sickly children?

Soon after the trip to Paris, another perfect solution seemed to present itself. On the southern coast of Lake Geneva, at the foot of Mont Blanc looking out toward Lausanne and the Swiss mountains, was the village of Thonon-les-Bains. A Protestant pastor was needed in this lovely Alpine countryside! André traveled there and introduced himself. Once again, he and the church council quickly reached an understanding. He was as good as selected.

But one woman on the council was absent. She was on her way to Paris, to the church offices. Then things took an inevitable turn. This plan too came to naught on the question of pacifism.

Was it a mistake to leave the work in Sin-le-Noble? Was it perhaps even "unspiritual"—a kind of escape? Magda and André began to doubt whether they were doing the right thing in their search for a new congregation. So they sought counsel from older, experienced acquaintances.

"You have made a commitment to give your lives in service to the church here in the north. If you leave, it would be an act of disobedience against God," said one assertive church leader.

"Since God has permitted your children to be sick, he is trying to tell you something: he wants you to move to another place," said two elderly women.

Considering the elderly women to be wiser, Magda and André followed their counsel and continued to look for another position. And, in the end, they found it, even though it was anything but an ideal congregation in an ideal location.

***

André's pacifist convictions, which had been the source of so many difficulties in France, led him to look outside the country to Germany, considered by many to be the archenemy. Since the time of his childhood, when he visited his relatives in Lippe, Germany, André had been in the homeland of his mother on only one other occasion. In the summer of 1927, he had participated in a conference of the International Fellowship of Reconciliation. Peace activists from nineteen countries had come together to express their opposition to the prevailing militarism and to advocate for the recognition of conscientious objection.

Now, five years later, he traveled again to Germany, this time for a peace march that began in France and was scheduled to pass through southern Germany. André was uneasy about the trip. Could he leave Magda and the four children alone in the summer house of the extended Trocmé family? But it was Magda who encouraged him: "Go ahead! You sometimes confuse duty with tradition. It's important that you leave behind a strong impression. The congregation is not going to collapse if you are gone for two weeks. And we aren't going to either."

The host and organizer of the gathering was the German Peace Federation, a coalition of groups with socialist tendencies. The federation had advertised the peace conference widely, and it filled halls in Frankfurt, Offenbach, and Heidelberg without any difficulty. In Offenbach, a pastor by the name of Goethe led the event. Shortly before the meeting, his home was trashed by young Nazis. The police openly colluded with the vandals, arriving at the scene only after the perpetrators had left.

In Heidelberg, André himself was attacked. "You want to lather [dupe] us so that France and England can shave us closer!" yelled a group of Brownshirts as one of them waved a revolver in André's face.[1] "Go ahead," André shouted. "Kill me here in front of all these people." And that was what calmed the man.

---

1 Brownshirts was another name for the Sturmabteilung (Storm Troopers), who served as the original paramilitary wing of the Nazi Party.

Only later did André discover that the young man had already murdered four Jews.

When participants in the peace march arrived in Reutlingen, the local coordinator greeted them with bad news. "The theater is already completely filled. But it's all Brownshirts. They have sworn not to allow you to speak. Unfortunately, we need to cancel the event."

At André's initiative, the group retreated for a prayer. Then they decided to go into the theater and at least try to speak to the Nazis. André, the foreigner who spoke the best German, was asked to speak to the crowd. The peace activists entered the theater through the stage entrance and stood quietly behind the curtain. On the other side they could hear the noise of the mob.

"The lectern is there in the front," counseled a person knowledgeable of the theater. "Go right to it and begin to speak immediately. Otherwise, you'll be shouted down before you're able to say a word."

André did exactly that. Scarcely had he reached the lectern when he greeted the crowd of four or five hundred people with the words "Germany, awaken!"

Quiet. A stunned silence.

"I mean exactly what I said," André continued. "Germany must awaken since we are now threatened once more with a world war. I'm French, and our people suffered the most during the last war. But now it's time to forgive each other and to be reconciled. Whoever here today is a Christian is against war and everything that promotes preparation for war. Christians will refuse military service."

Thunderous applause. Was he dreaming? Or were these Nazis really applauding a pacifist?

In any case, the following speakers were able to present what they had prepared without interruption.

"You said exactly the same thing that our führer said!" the commander of the Reutlinger Sturmabteilung said to André after the event. "Justice and equality for everyone! Peace!"

"Yes, but Hitler says it a little bit differently," André said. "And why does he persecute the Jews?"

"Jews are the biggest enemy of peace," the young commander said. He could not be dissuaded from this conviction.

"I have often thought back on that scene in Reutlingen," wrote André years later. "Hitler succeeded in inspiring guileless young people for his malicious intentions. To the irreligious, critical, and sharp-witted French, the naiveté of the Germans—their simple-minded tendencies in both good and evil, their impulse to muddle together all values—was always incomprehensible."

A few months later, Adolf Hitler came to power. But he did not exactly "seize" power, as some describe it. Rather, he was promoted from president to chancellor in a completely legal, democratic manner. He received overwhelming support from enthusiastic masses who were, and who wished to remain, unaware.

***

André was back in France and still looking for a new position. When he finally heard of a place where people supposedly wanted him as a pastor, and where it was guaranteed that there would be no problems with the church administration, he and Magda had to search long and hard for it on the map.

French maps identified fourteen different places bearing the name Chambon—the word comes from the Latin *campus*, or field—and apparently there were fields everywhere. To distinguish the various Chambons from each other, many of them had an additional name as well. So Magda and André searched for Le Chambon-sur-Lignon. But, confusingly, some maps marked the same place as

Chambon-de-Tence. They finally found the Lignon, a tributary of the Loire River in the Massif Central not far from Ardèche, which helped them locate the correct Chambon. Unfortunately, it appeared to be quite far from any other attractive destinations. What a remote region! Not quite part of the Cévennes mountain range, but also not part of Provence; not in western France nor quite in eastern France, and difficult to reach from the Rhône valley because it was a thousand meters (about three thousand feet) above the river. André could already imagine the handful of Protestant farmers who probably lived there. The region was known as the

Le Chambon-sur-Lignon is located in south-central France.

plateau Vivarais-Lignon. Not exactly memorable (later they would become accustomed to simply saying "the plateau" as everyone else did). In fact, there was only one recognizable name on the map: the Loire River, whose source must have been located somewhere in the mountains not far from Le Chambon.

"I had promised myself," André wrote, "never to become a village pastor. It was the cities and their problems that fascinated me." But what could he do? Stay in Sin-le-Noble for the foreseeable future and consign his children to an unhealthy climate? His reputation among church administrators was evidently so bad that he really could not expect anything better than a village like Le Chambon. It was only a question of yes or no. André thought about his children: Nelly, Jean-Pierre, Jacques, and Daniel. With a sigh, he said yes.

But even here a trick was needed so that André could be hired without once again having the rug pulled out from beneath him. René, a friend from his student days, was now president of the church district and wanted to help his old friend. It was his idea that André should serve in Le Chambon as the interim pastor for a transition period of one year. No one was going to go to the work of standing in the way of that arrangement. And then, after a year had gone by, they could see where things stood.

André agreed to the strategy. He had only one request in the matter: the parsonage at Le Chambon needed to be equipped with central heating. Their home would be nearly a thousand meters (about three thousand feet) above sea level, and he and Magda did not want to begin their day for nine months of the year by trying to start a fire in the kitchen and the workroom.

In September 1934, after a journey of eight hundred kilometers (five hundred miles), the Trocmé family arrived at their new home. They took one look and turned away. The heating had not yet been installed, and it was already cold. The parsonage, a ramshackle castle built out of coarse granite on a slope overlook-ing the Lignon, was a construction site. So the Trocmés moved into an apartment for an expensive wait that stretched their fi-nances to the breaking point.

At least Le Chambon, with its nearly one thousand inhab-itants, had hotels and apartments for rent—in great quantity. Located at the north edge of the plateau was Saint-Étienne, a center of metal production known especially for its weapons and tools. But coal was also in great supply in Saint-Étienne. Since the end of the nineteenth century, Le Chambon had become a kind of health resort for the miners, and even more so for their children. A single-track railroad extended into the plateau—a tiny spur line that brought workers' children up the mountain to seek respite for their health. Before they were parceled out to the hotels, apartments, and convalescent homes, the children were required to stand on a scale situated by the track in front of the tiny train station. Here the weight of every child was carefully noted—and then compared with the outcome a few weeks later, ideally with a significant gain. Only then could a child climb back into the train for the return trip home.

So Le Chambon was the center of an early form of tourism and a modest hotel industry. "But there was nothing of the hospi-tality that we knew in the north," noted André. "What we had in Le Chambon was tourism as a kind of industry."

Was there a bit of bitterness in his tone? This time, at least, Magda and André were free from any illusions right from the start.

Only three families in the village could lay claim to a bit of culture: Dr. Riou and his wife; Madame de Félice, an elderly, rich, witty landowner; and Mademoiselle Matile, who had founded a convalescent home for children. The Darcissac couple, both teachers in the elementary school, were quite unique, but their perspective did not extend beyond the plateau. Madame

Marion, the widow of a former pastor who ran a boarding house, was a busy bee, but not much more than that.

Is the person who writes such things arrogant? Or is he simply a clear-minded, analytical observer? In any case, André operated out of the definitions of "culture" that were popular in his time. Naturally, André never would have spoken these thoughts aloud. Indeed, he made these notations years later, perhaps only to cleanse his soul or as a storehouse of memories for his children and grandchildren.

In the Picardie region, André's homeland in northern France, farmers were called *cultivateurs*, since they "cultivated," or refined, that which the earth brought forth. Here, they were simply called farmers. "With the onset of fall, a sort of agricultural heaviness descended on everything around here," André wrote. "The plateau proved to be a hostile corner of the world, from which the farmer could feed himself only with great effort. Now winter began, and it would last for the next nine months. The distillation of

The village of Le Chambon-sur-Lignon, situated on a plateau in south-central France. Chambon Foundation.

all human wisdom here was expressed in the saying 'Nine months of winter; three months of drudgery.'"

Winters here "at the end of the earth," as André sometimes called it, were simply a matter of survival. The miners' children who had been sent to the countryside around Le Chambon for health reasons were sent back to Saint-Étienne. The window shops of the hotels and most of the boarding houses were boarded up. Anyone who might have made some money as a hotelier tried to hide it from his neighbors in order to comport with the general complaints of the farmers. Lousy weather; lousy harvest; lousy health.

Nevertheless, there was one good thing about the winter: after all the work in the short agricultural season, the people of Le Chambon attended church again. What else did they have to do?

And besides, there was a new pastor . . .

14

Descendants of Refugees

Le Chambon, 1934

Even though the Protestant church in the little village of Le Chambon was unusually large, it was filled to the last pew. In striking large letters above the door were the words *Aimez-vous les uns les autres*: Love one another.

Moving through the door of the vestibule into the actual sanctuary, churchgoers found themselves standing under a bright vaulted ceiling, and they knew immediately what truly mattered in this large space. To the right, benches; to the left, benches; and in the middle, an aisle that led to the pulpit. For it is the Word and nothing but the Word that matters most to Reformed Christians. No decorated altar, no flowers, no paintings. Statues of saints or a crucifix would be unthinkable. There was not even a simple wooden cross.

The wall behind the pulpit was not entirely bare: on each side, to the left and the right, was a wooden panel with the numbers for the hymns that were to be sung in the worship service. But the message of the space, today just as much as in the fall of 1934

when André led his first worship service there, was clear: Look at
the pulpit and listen!

How did it come about that here in this village of a thousand inhabitants, nestled in deeply Catholic France, a Protestant
church could attract several hundred members? How was it that
more than half the people attending church lived not even in the
village itself but in distant and scattered farmsteads, which meant
that attending church required great effort?

*The Protestant church building (sometimes called "the temple") in
Le Chambon in contemporary times. Hanna Schott.*

The answer is rooted in the dramatic history of French Protestantism. Like almost all the other inhabitants of the plateau, most Chambonnais—which is what the residents of Le Chambon were called—were descendants of refugees. As the central ideas of the Reformation reached France in the early sixteenth century, those people who turned from the Catholic faith were called Huguenots. Although the name's origin is unclear, it possibly comes from an old word for "confederation"—a reference to the Swiss Confederation. Initially, being Swiss and being Protestant seemed to be virtually one and the same thing. It was, after all, John Calvin (who was actually French, but was active in Geneva) who brought the "heresy" to France. To be French meant that one was Catholic. And this "self-evident" fact was defended with the sword.

The bloody persecution of the Protestants lasted sixty years, and increasingly took on the character of a civil war. In 1598, the Edict of Nantes granted Huguenots freedom of religion even as it held firm to the principle that Catholicism was, and would remain, the state religion. By that time, thousands of Protestants had fled France. The halfhearted guarantee of religious tolerance—which was not binding, for example, in Paris—secured a tenuous peace for almost ninety years. Then, in 1685, the edict was revoked. Louis XIV, the so-called Sun King, pursued a mixed policy of conversion and persecution in order to bring Protestants back to the true path of Catholicism. The result was yet another wave of refugees. And it was not only the poor and uneducated who fled the country. Overrepresented among the roughly two hundred thousand people who found refuge in Switzerland, the Netherlands, Germany, Scandinavia, England, and North America were well-trained, literate craftspeople. The ancestors of André's mother were among these refugees.

Most of the Protestants who remained in France lived in the countryside, or had been forced to flee there. They were not as educated and had either missed the opportunity to leave or had chosen not to do so. In many cases, they found themselves now in villages without pastors, since nearly all the Protestant theologians had left the country. In Huguenot history, this period is known as *le désert*, "the desert." Even today the Huguenot museum in the Cévennes bears the name Musée du Désert—Desert Museum—although it is in the middle of a green forest. When the biblically grounded Huguenots said "desert," they were thinking of how the children of Israel wandered for forty difficult years between Egypt and the Promised Land. It was a good thing that the French Protestants had no clue that their own wandering in the desert would last 250 years. Not until the French Revolution were they finally granted unconditional rights of citizenship. (That the same revolution then initiated a kind of desert wandering for the Catholic church is another sad story.)

Many of the persecuted Huguenots found refuge in the region around Le Chambon. Here, high on the desolate, forested plateau, they hoped no one would find them. Here they broke the sod, carved out an austere existence, and preserved their faith. To do this, they remained secluded, marrying almost exclusively within their group. (This gave Magda and André the advantage of only needing to remember six different family names, which almost without exception were first names—Abel, Hénoch, Rachel—taken from the Old Testament.) These families expected nothing from the world except to be left in peace.

Yet even this simple wish was not always granted them. On several occasions, the king's infantry rode into the village and arrested the pastor and several church members. Sometimes the prisoners were hanged or burned alive in Le Chambon; sometimes they were first taken to Montpellier or Le Puy before being executed. After this sudden horror, things would be peaceful again, but for how long, no one knew.

View of mountains of the Massif Central. Hanna Schott.

Even after the French Revolution permitted Protestants to move about freely and to practice their faith openly, the Chambonnais remained exactly as they were. The frugal Huguenot farmers had become accustomed to the hardships of life in the austere landscape, and they knew that they could only expect trouble from the world around them. So why should they leave the plateau?

When André became the pastor, some 95 percent of the inhabitants of Le Chambon were still Protestant. The congregation numbered no more, but also no fewer, souls than it had three hundred years earlier.

One thing had changed: several of the Protestants in the region had adopted the teachings of an English minister who traveled and preached throughout much of Europe, as well as in North America, Australia, and New Zealand, during the second half of the nineteenth century. John Nelson Darby, a former Anglican priest, was an original, idiosyncratic interpreter of the Bible. His followers became known as Darbyites. The Darbyites separated themselves from the Reformed Church and met in their own private gatherings. They rejected the idea that the church should be led by theologically trained pastors—professionals who, in a certain sense, always stood over the laity. Instead, they tried to move toward their ideal of a congregation of equal "brothers." (They were not so convinced of the equality of the sisters.) If conservative Protestants from the plateau were biblically rooted and especially familiar with the Old Testament, then the Darbyites were even more zealous. The Darbyites often did not even take the trouble of quoting a biblical text; it was enough to simply cite the chapter and verse. They all knew many of these passages by memory, so chapter and verse sufficed to communicate what a person was thinking. Thus, if one simply said, "First Timothy 2:9," the other person knew what was meant: namely, that a woman was wearing a hat which was not appropriate for a Sunday morning gathering.

***

Even though the Darbyites did not attend André's sermons that fall, they naturally turned a critical eye to the new pastor. André was now thirty-three years old. He had seven years' experience as a congregational leader, he had been married for eight years, and he was the father of four children. Almost nothing of that shy, mumbling student who was perpetually red with embarrassment was still recognizable. One exception, perhaps, was his posture. In almost all the pictures from this period, his head is tilted slightly to the side, as if he could prevent himself from appearing too tall.

But his fear of standing in front of people and speaking freely had disappeared completely. According to his brother Francis, André became a "gifted pulpit speaker" during his time in Le

André Trocmé holding the hand of his daughter, Nelly, and walking with members of the congregation in Le Chambon. Private collection.

Chambon. His clear, full voice filled the sanctuary—not a small matter in the decades before the installation of church sound systems. "His authority exceeded that of anyone I ever heard preach," wrote Francis, astonished by his younger brother. "He began in a simple, unforced manner with current events or religious reflections. Then he gradually increased his tempo, expounding on the theme with his own feelings and thoughts, confessing his conscience with an evocative clarity and rectitude. He spoke in the idiom of the people, sometimes even using coarse language."

Still, a few sentences later, Francis recalled, "Look how he would direct us to the highest peak of religious thoughts and let us hover there, truly rapt. Then, lovingly, he led us back to the earth and joined us all in a feeling of peace, so that the last word, 'Amen,' was filled with the true meaning of the word—so be it. At the end, we sat there, tears in our eyes, as if we had just been listening to music that stirred our deepest emotions."

As André came down from the elevated pulpit to sit again in the first pew, church members would often exchange slow, knowing nods. During the opening sentences of most of André's sermons, congregants would have noted each other's wrinkled brows. To their ears, the message sometimes sounded suspiciously like the Social Gospel.[1] But maybe that was only a quirk that the young man had picked up in America, something that he would soon get out of his system. What followed was solid biblical teaching, and they could be reassured and lean back again in their pews.

Then, with the closing hymn they all knew by memory—"La Cévenole," the hymn of the Huguenots—the service would come to a close. "La Cévenole" was a mixture of patriotic anthem, hero hymn, martyr commemoration, and chorale. It extolled the Cévennes, the mountains to the south of Le Chambon, which had offered a refuge for thousands of Huguenots ("Greetings to you, beloved mountains!"); praised the courageous Protestants who had refused to bow to their persecutors ("What manner of blood flows through your veins, what love in your hearts?"); and strengthened them to follow in the footsteps of their great exemplars ("Spirit, which gave them life, inspire now your children"). The text itself did not originate in the time of the bloody conflict itself, but rather was relatively new. Written for the two hundredth anniversary commemoration of the revocation of the Edict of Nantes, the hymn was first sung in 1885. So when André Trocmé joined in the song with his new congregation, the hymn was barely fifty years old. From the deep perspective of church history, this favorite anthem was in the category of new congregational hymns.

---

1 The Social Gospel was a prominent approach to Christian ethics in early twentieth-century America that called Christians to prioritize action on issues such as poverty, crime, racism, educational inequality, and war.

Is the God of our fathers
not also forever our God?
Let us serve him in these good days,
as they did when days were bad.

Yes, the members of the church in Le Chambon were living in good days. With this awareness, the congregation would leave the church building in good spirits. André and Magda would stand in the courtyard in the mild fall sun, breathe in the fresh mountain air, and warmly greet the churchgoers.

Perhaps it had indeed been a good idea for them to move to the countryside. If things remained the way they were now, the years ahead for their family and ministry would be peaceful ones. They would serve God in these good days, and they would grow accustomed to the sleepy calm of village life.

15

A School of Resistance

Le Chambon, 1935–1938

The years in rural seclusion could have been pleasant. The Trocmés enjoyed living in a large parsonage, with its great view of the Lignon River: in summer a babbling brook, in winter a rushing river. And as they had hoped, here the children were gaining weight and developing robust health by playing with the village children in the woods and stream in all kinds of weather.

But the Trocmés were the wrong sort of people for this sort of life. Magda and André did not care to pull back, tend to their idyllic parsonage, and hope that the church administrators would forget all about the "Trocmé case." To the contrary. They recognized in short order the problems and the opportunities of their setting. And they were determined to use their particular gifts to influence and shape Le Chambon.

The problem was that the Chambonnais did not always receive new ideas favorably. Whoever found life in Le Chambon lacking could leave the town and region, and most who stayed

André and Magda Trocmé and their children (from left) Daniel, Jacques, Jean-Pierre, and Nelly in front of the parsonage at Le Chambon. Private collection.

were happy with the way things had always been. Naturally, those who left were the young people and the intellectually curious, including all those who wished to receive more than a grade school education.

But there were opportunities too, including the steady coming and going of the "outsiders," especially the many children who came to the village for their health. In addition, there was the incalculable resource of the Huguenot tradition—namely, a collective memory of a time when they themselves were searching for protection and hospitality.

Within this constellation of problems and opportunities lay enormous possibilities. André recognized this as clearly as Magda. But it was Magda who had the dazzling idea: "Let's start a school!"

***

Magda already had a model in mind. In 1921, as a nineteen-year-old, Magda had been to a health resort in Torre Pellice, the center of the Waldensian Church in the far northern Italian region of Piemonte. There she had become acquainted with a school, the Collegio di Torre Pellice, that was exactly the kind of school that she now imagined for Le Chambon. Boys and girls were instructed together in the same classroom, which was a new idea for many. The school had a clear Protestant Christian orientation combined with a broad openness to the world. Above all, the school in Torre Pellice was a secondary school. If the children of the miners in Piemonte could receive higher education and the parents there could accept the idea of their children receiving more schooling, then why shouldn't the idea at least be tried in Le Chambon?

In 1936, André organized the first meeting of all those he thought might be supportive of the idea to establish a school. It would be a sort of planning conference for Le Chambon and the surrounding countryside. Participants were invited to freely share their wishes and ideas for such a school.

"Wouldn't a kind of Huguenot academy—a Protestant cultural center—be possible?" asked the head of the bookstore.

"We really need an international summer camp, like the YMCA camps in the United States," insisted the mayor, who was a former pastor from Switzerland.

"We have to move beyond the blinders of nationalistic education and instruct children in the spirit of peace, the spirit of the gospel." This, naturally, was André's biggest wish.

"But there's also a lot of room for improvement in the way that we run the health spas for the foreign children," offered the town doctor.

"Now, slowly," said André, scarcely able to conceal his joy. No one here had dismissed the idea as complete nonsense. "We will make an application to the synod," he said. "First we'll focus on a school, a church school. But we need to have a position approved; we will need a principal for the school."

"Yes, our plans need to be recognized by the state too," the mayor said. "And above all, we need to find people who are willing to come to Le Chambon." He sighed. Perhaps the somewhat ludicrous plans of the pastor could help to stem the flow of people out of his town.

***

The first year in Le Chambon was long past, and then the second and third as well. No one spoke any longer of an interim or transitional period for the Trocmés. They belonged to Le Chambon— that was clear. Even the church administrators recognized this. Things were happening in this congregation. This "dangerous and difficult André Trocmé"—as he was described in a document written by the church president—had plainly made his peace with his "exile to the countryside." In his zeal, André had quickly taken on even more work. Now he was seeking some relief, in the form of an assistant pastor who could also serve as headmaster of the school.

The first candidate was sent to the village for an introduction. But when he realized that he was to be simultaneously a pastor and the schoolmaster, and just how uncertain the entire project was, he withdrew without delay.

André himself then took the initiative and invited someone he knew to interview at the parsonage. Edouard Theis was a theology student who had held the tutoring position with the Rockefellers before André's tenure. In the ensuing years, Edouard had married Mildred, an American, and had worked as a missionary in Cameroon and Madagascar. He was the father of six daughters (at the time, Mildred was pregnant again with another girl, and an eighth daughter would later be born at Le Chambon).

Edouard was also a member of the International Fellowship of Reconciliation and, like André, had rejected military service for reasons of conscience. Now, years later, they met again and found each other to be brothers in spirit. André explained what he had in mind and noted immediately that Edouard, who had traveled around the world, was not easily shocked. Edouard accepted that he would have a half-time position with the congregation and would work half-time as the teacher of Latin, Greek, and French in a school that had not yet been established and that did not yet have any classrooms. He saw that it was still unclear whom his colleagues would be and that the financing of the whole thing was still on very shaky footing. The matter was settled.

As the congregation soon discovered, Edouard was not someone who sought the limelight. He simply wanted to be somewhere where his gifts could be used, and that seemed to be precisely the case in Le Chambon. He was a large, calm man who was compelled by his office to speak in public but did so without rhetorical flourish and always in a very soft voice. He could completely lose himself in the songs and the prayer of a worship service in which he was supposed to preach. Sometimes someone would have to nudge him. "Oh yes, of course; I'm the pastor," he would murmur, and then walk up to the pulpit.

***

In September 1938, the École Nouvelle Cévenole (New Cévenole School) opened its doors. Actually, *doors* is a bit exaggerated, since the door of the school opened into a single classroom in the multipurpose room directly behind the church sanctuary. Here eighteen students sat in chairs behind newly constructed desks. The furniture maker of the city was eager to support the new school and had built the chairs and desks.

Edouard Theis—who from this day forward served not only as a pastor in the village but also as a principal—already had three colleagues. His wife, Mildred, served as the English teacher; Magda Trocmé taught Italian; and a Ms. Höfert was the German teacher. With native speakers offering instruction in foreign languages, the school was well situated to develop a strong international orientation. The students would have to attend the village school for the subjects the school could not yet offer. Over time, additional teachers and classrooms would be found. And, hopefully, financing as well, since not all instructors would be willing to teach without remuneration as the two pastors' wives did.

That a school located not in the Cévennes claimed the name "New Cévenole School" was the source of irritation to some.[1] But the appropriateness of the name was made evident in the very first year of the school's existence. The name was not intended as a description of a geographical location but rather as an identity with a tradition. The intention was to take as a model the "spirit of the Cévennes"—that is, the strength of resistance and the pious stubbornness of the Huguenots.

And, almost immediately, the opportunity arose to demonstrate exactly that.

***

Ms. Höfert, the German teacher, served as the first involuntary example. The Austrian had been living in Le Chambon for only six months. When German soldiers marched across the Austrian

---

1 The Cévennes is the mountain range just to the south of Le Chambon. Located near the Massif Central, an elevated region in southern France, these were the mountains that provided protection to many French Huguenots fleeing persecution.

border, she had instantly recognized what the *Anschluss* (alignment) between Austria and the German Reich would mean for her as a Jew. Overnight, she was forced to abandon her homeland and orient herself to the west. Thus she was one of the first persons to claim Le Chambon as a place of refuge during this time.

But Ms. Höfert was not the very first. Since the summer of 1936, troops supporting the elected government in Spain had been fighting against a military coup led by General Franco. Not long thereafter, the first democrats were forced to flee for their lives. Several of them came to Le Chambon.

But why Le Chambon? Why not some other desolate village where one could also easily disappear? The answer is not obvious even these many decades later. Probably it was simply because of the stories and rumors that were then in circulation. Already in 1914, at the beginning of World War I, some Alsatian soldiers, their homeland trapped between the two fronts, had fled to Le Chambon. Somewhere in the village, people had provided them with accommodations, and no one turned them in to the military. These facts were not noted in travel books, but word got around somehow. Evidently, there was a certain defiance toward the state associated with "the spirit of the Cévennes," and this knowledge was stored in the back of people's minds throughout Europe.

More than anyone could have imagined, the École Nouvelle Cévenole grew rapidly, and it became even more internationally oriented than any plan might have predicted. By the second school year, enrollment had risen from 18 students to 40; in the third year, to 150; and in the fourth year, 1941–42, 250 students were somehow accommodated and instructed. Children from the village had quickly become a minority, and more than a few teachers themselves had to first learn French, the language in which they taught.

Indeed, many teachers were also refugees, just like many of the children. No one could complain about the academic standards, even though efforts to receive state accreditation for the school were unsuccessful in the first year, as the teachers could not yet formally verify the necessary credentials. By the second year, a French professor, who had been dismissed from a university because he was Jewish, was teaching the French courses.

The physical setting of the school was quite basic. Magda taught her few Italian students throughout the summer in the bathroom of a woman from the village; during the winter, she taught in the empty rooms of a hotel that had been closed for the season (the only downside was that the rooms were not heated). The original plan to expand the school systematically, adding an additional grade level each year as the original students grew older, proved to be impossible. The newcomers never arrived promptly at the beginning of a new school year, nor did their ages match the necessary grade levels, since their academic preparation was as varied as their family backgrounds. The students comprised a motley crew, and the teachers did as well. Over time, everyone adjusted. Magda found special pleasure in giving older students a crash course in Italian whenever they needed an additional foreign language for their university entrance exam. For emergency cases, she gave individual instruction, often in the kitchen of the parsonage while she was preparing supper and tending to her own children.

***

Whoever took part in this kind of education never forgot it for the rest of their lives. Joseph Atlas, a young Jewish man from Warsaw, came with his mother and brother to France even before the Germans attacked the country. Anti-Semitism in Poland was reason enough to emigrate. "In the school, I spoke Polish and German with my friends," Joseph recalled. "French was already challenging enough, but then I was lacking a second foreign language as one of my test subjects for the university entrance exam. Magda decided that I needed to learn Italian. What should I do? I became her student. I have never forgotten her rather antiauthoritarian approach to pedagogy, or her explanations of the poems of Leopardi and the comedies of Goldoni."[2]

Was it crucial that a young Polish Jew, whose life was being threatened by racism, know who Leopardi and Goldoni were? And should he spend his time interpreting their work?

For the teachers of the École Cévenole, the clear answer was yes. The teachers at Le Chambon wanted to educate their charges in the ways of peace. Children in neighboring countries were becoming mentally and physically armed and ready for war. Already at the age of ten, they were joining the "youth movement" or the "young girls club" and learning watchwords like *battle*, *attack*, *austerity*, and *toughness*.

Peace cannot be learned like Latin vocabulary words, and reconciliation cannot be taught with lecture notes and homework. Yet the teachers at Le Chambon were committed to helping students learn the ways of peace during an era in which those ways were being fast forgotten.

---

2 Giacomo Leopardi was an Italian poet, philosopher, and radical thinker in the nineteenth century; Carlo Osvaldo Goldoni was an eighteenth-century Italian playwright and librettist with an aversion to church hypocrisy and intolerance.

16

A Stranger
and You Took Me In

Le Chambon, 1939–40

The woman collapsed into a chair at the large table in Magda's kitchen. This was the legendary scene: Magda at home with the children on a wintry evening when the doorbell rang. This was not the first act of welcome in Le Chambon during those difficult days, but it marked the beginning of a new stage in the drama that would unfold over the next few years.

Magda warmed leftovers from supper. She took the damp sandals and placed them close to the fire and then went upstairs to prepare a bed for the night. Undoubtedly, the woman was not in a position to travel any farther this evening.

When Magda returned to the kitchen, she smelled the sharp aroma of something burning. Using the poker, Magda pulled the smoldering sandals away from the coals. The exhausted woman had not noticed that they had slipped into the fire.

"Don't worry about a thing," Magda said. "Those sandals weren't good for this weather in any case. Tomorrow I'll make sure that you get a new pair of shoes."

To find a pair of shoes in a common size in Le Chambon could not be too difficult. The next morning, Magda set out. Since the start of the war, everything was rationed, including shoes—one pair per year per person—so it would not be possible to buy new ones. But Magda was certain that some family would have an extra pair tucked away in a closet. And that was indeed the case: a young couple had a pair that more or less fit the woman's feet. Problem solved.

The search for shoes proved to be a pivotal experience for Magda. It made clear to her just how much life in France had changed during the last six months. And she was beginning to recognize, going forward, how much was going to change in her life and in the life of the village. How much would *have* to change.

***

On June 14, 1940, German troops marched into Paris. Two days later, the western advance came to an end. For the signing of the Franco-German Armistice on June 22, the parties recovered from a museum the famous railroad dining car in which the Germans had acknowledged their defeat in 1918. They put the train car on the tracks at the exact spot in the forest of Compiègne, not far from André's childhood home, where the Germans had surrendered years earlier. Now it was the French who were surrendering. The Germans were glad to call attention to this historical location.

Indeed, the armistice marked France's full surrender. The country was divided in two: the north and west portions of France, about 60 percent of the total country, were now under

German occupation. The remaining portion, in the south, the so-called Free Zone, lost its autonomy, although it remained under French administration. Vichy, a resort town in the Auvergne, became the home of the new government. There, the Germans essentially appointed the eighty-four-year-old Philippe Pétain to rule as head of state.

Le Chambon was two hundred kilometers (more than one hundred miles) south of Vichy and therefore part of the Free Zone. But what did *free* actually mean? Beginning in October, an order came into effect for all of France, not merely for the occupied zone, that all Jews were to be handed over to German officials. All of them! French, German, Austrian, and Polish refugees—no matter who, no matter where.

Consequently, many Jews fled southward. Here they were not so directly under German control. Here, they hoped, things would be better.

***

Magda hurried through the village. She often hurried, a habit that many residents in Le Chambon liked about her. Magda was always there, always approachable, always eager for a chat at the market, ready to offer advice and quick to find practical solutions. She often spoke loudly, with an unmistakably rough voice, and always fast, with an accent that betrayed her Italian homeland even though she had lived in France for many years. A few people were troubled by the fact that she was often very direct and said exactly what she was thinking instead of spending time on polite niceties. Others appreciated that they always knew exactly where they stood with Magda.

Now she was once again on the move for a charitable mission, this time on behalf of a Jewish woman whose shoes had been placed too close to the fire. And while she was on her mission, she began to ask herself who might be able to take in the unexpected guest for a short time. It was impossible to do so in the parsonage. To supplement André's meager income, the Trocmés had already freed up two rooms to rent to students, who lived and ate with the family. Moreover, since food was now being rationed, she could support an additional mouth at the table for a day or two, but not longer.

"So in all innocence, I went to the courthouse and told my story to the representative of the mayor, since the mayor himself, Mr. Guillon, was gone at the moment," Magda recalled later.

I thought that he could help me. But instead he became upset. This would be completely impossible; there were already more than enough French Jews, and I really should not bother myself now with German Jews, since that brought the entire village into danger. He wanted me to send this woman away. Imagine that— send her away! Where to? I was desperate.

So I continued on my way to another important person—a French Jewish woman who was in Le Chambon because the cities had become too dangerous for Jews. I explained to her that I had a Jewish woman in my home, that I wasn't sure if she could stay, and that I needed her help. And, as in the mayor's office, I was not only rebuffed, but I had to listen to yet another scolding: the flood of foreign Jews was only further endangering French Jews!

I was completely demoralized. We had to think of something. And so we finally ended up resorting to the underground, with false papers, false photos, false names . . . with lies.

Find the place where you can do what is necessary and right— for Magda, the matter was clear: the parsonage and the school were precisely the places where she and André could do good. Now, since the beginning of the war, this was truer than ever.

André, by contrast, was filled with doubts about whether he could, or should, remain in Le Chambon. During the first days of the war, he had assumed he would be conscripted into the army. Refusing to bear arms in this situation would be quite different from his time in Morocco. Back then, France had not been under serious threat. But now his decision would be put to an extremely hard test. Shortly thereafter, however, he learned that married men eligible for conscription would have two years added to their age for each child in their family. This meant that, on paper, he was suddenly eight years older and thus too old for regular military service. In the same way, his colleague Edouard Theis, father of eight daughters, added sixteen years to his age. Assuming nothing extraordinary happened, this meant that both men would be spared deployment to the front. But did this also mean that their place during the war should be in Le Chambon?

André agonized over this question, sometimes alone in his study and sometimes with Magda on Mondays, which was his day off. On those days he and Magda went for long walks, putting as much distance as possible between themselves and Le Chambon, where it was never easy to speak with each other in peace. He had promised never to make any decisions without her.

***

A half year before the Jewish woman showed up at their door, André had felt inwardly torn as he developed plans and then watched as his initiatives came to naught.

On September 5, 1939, he had written a formal statement, albeit mostly for himself, titled "A Clarification of My Position at the Time of the War." The war had not yet reached France, but André had no illusions. In the lengthy report, André summarized his life up until that point, making it clear how his coming of age so close to the battles of the Great War had led him to his pacifist convictions. "I have served my fatherland to the best of my abilities as a teacher of young people—serving first the children of workers and then children in the countryside," André wrote. "I am still prepared today to serve my fatherland with all my power—as long as it does not demand of me what God forbids me to do: namely, to participate in a war."

In the middle of his account, André saw far into the future, as if the view from his workroom window not only revealed the gentle rise on the other side of the Lignon but somehow extended far beyond the horizon. "I think that some people are intended to have a special fate," he wrote. "Their life is predetermined, completely independently of what they themselves desire. (After all, one doesn't choose his own mother.) They must face this fate until the very end—and, in so doing, attempt to submit joyfully to God's will."

But what did that mean? For André's pastorate? For the school? Clearly, André was thinking now about specific people who would someday read the pages he now was filling. He was offering future readers a few things regarding his person and his role that could be consulted at a later point to challenge any rumors or assumptions.

I am a servant who obeyed orders from the time I was a child. I have no interest in eccentricities. I have never had visions. Everything is in order regarding my life and my mental state. I am not an extraordinary person. I have a wife, four children, and concerns about material things. I suffer from all the flaws and weaknesses of character that others do. I do not regard myself as better than anyone else. Like all people, I also bear my part of the responsibility for the start of wars. I do not excuse Hitler— he embodies precisely the evil that I abhor. I do not blame Daladier or Chamberlain, since I don't know what I would have done in their place.[1] I have not prevented a single soldier from taking up his post: my responsibilities as pastor would not have allowed me to do so, and I have too much respect for the individual conscience. Already long ago I refrained from organizing any sort of public peace demonstrations, since the only thing that truly counts in such important matters is one's own example. For fifteen years I have belonged to the International Peace Alliance [Internationalen Friedensbund], but not to any political party. I am freed from allegiances on all sides—but not from God.

I do not want to remain behind the front in domestic security. I ask only that I might be able to take risks in serving those who are the most pitiful victims of war: the women and children of bombed-out cities. This service, however, must be exclusively as a civilian. I would be happy if, in so doing, I could give my life like others without being untrue to my master, Jesus Christ. God help me!

André folded the pages together, put them in an envelope, and gave them to Madame Marion, a friend of Magda's, for safekeeping. During a war, everything was possible, including a search of the parsonage.

Two days later, André wrote a letter to Marc Boegner. Since 1938, Boegner had been the president of the Union of Reformed Churches in France. "I want to inform you that regardless of my military usefulness, I have come to the certain conviction that God has called me to another place," André wrote. "I am certain that I am not fleeing from danger; instead, quite to the contrary, I wish to serve women, children, and the elderly in a city or

---

1 In September 1938, French prime minister Édouard Daladier and British prime minister Neville Chamberlain struck a deal with Hitler and Mussolini that came to be known as the Munich Agreement. This so-called policy of appeasement, which Daladier and Chamberlain hoped would avoid war, is today widely regarded as a failure.

bombed-out village as a civilian: either as a medic or as a caregiver in some sort of passive defense."

The presbytery of his congregation was informed of André's plans. "Whatever you do, we will continue to regard you as our pastor," the lay leaders assured him. André passed that message along in his letter to the president.

A month later André received a reply from Boegner.

My dear colleague,

Your letter moved me deeply. You surely will understand that I do not want to get caught up in a debate with you regarding what I, along with nearly all your colleagues, regard as a significant error in your interpretation of Holy Scriptures as well as Christian doctrine. I merely want to assure you that I will do everything within my power to ensure that you and all those who share your convictions will be put into a setting where you can demonstrate that you are not afraid. It is good that you offered your resignation from the pastorate.

What a strange letter. What was it supposed to mean?

André Trocmé wearing his clerical collar and holding his Bible. Photo taken during the war. Chambon Foundation.

The residents of Le Chambon wanted their pastor to stay. The military, at least at the outset, did not require his services. And Boegner did not expressly state that André could *not* serve any longer as a pastor. So during the winter of 1939–40, André remained, at least for the time being, in Le Chambon.

But then circumstances changed. In the spring of 1940, the war, which up until then had been focused only on eastern Europe, shifted to the west: Belgium, the Netherlands, and France. The country was in motion. André and Edouard reported as volunteers to the American Red Cross, with support from Marc Boegner and a letter of recommendation from John D. Rockefeller. They traveled to Lyon to present themselves in person—where they were promptly rejected by the Red Cross. Two men, with twelve children between them, were far too expensive. To be sure, the two had offered to serve as volunteers. But who wanted to be responsible for bringing two families into a crisis, one that could easily be avoided if the fathers simply remained at home and went about their normal work?

Downcast, André and Edouard returned to the village. Their heroism was not in demand.

Nor was their sacrifice.

Or was it?

***

In March 1939, a half year before the beginning of the war, André had written a remarkably prescient article. He was required to take his turn contributing a column for a regional paper of the Reformed Church. Although no one could have yet predicted the precarious situation that would soon develop in Europe, André was already calling on his readers to express their solidarity with the victims of National Socialist ideology in neighboring countries.

"Therefore, you are to love those who are foreigners, for you yourselves were foreigners in Egypt."

This admonition to the Israelites (Deuteronomy 10:19) is noteworthy for its relevance even today, for it speaks directly to us as Reformed Christians, who, though perhaps not in a physical sense, are direct spiritual descendants of the Huguenots who were persecuted and forced to flee in the seventeenth and eighteenth centuries.

Now once again people are being persecuted in the most horrific ways: hundreds of thousands of Christians, Jews, and democrats are trying to escape oppression and violence. Yet only a small portion of the persecuted even have the possibility of fleeing, since many of them have no possessions whatsoever and the free countries are barely cracking open their doors. We deny work permits to the majority who are seeking refuge here; we condemn them to idleness and often to homelessness. Some of them find themselves in prison right now because of a clear and repugnant crime: they no longer wished to beg and go hungry and therefore are guilty of working. Others, despairing, have indeed been misled into criminality or the insanity of suicide.

In the midst of the brutality and the indifference of our context, we as Christians are now being asked if we will hear the voice of the Master and Savior: "For I was hungry and you gave me something to eat. I was thirsty and you gave me to drink. I was a stranger, and you took me in."

The task was at hand. And it was really quite clear.

17

The Weapons of the Spirit

Le Chambon, 1940

How does a Protestant preacher, raised by the strictest of principles, teach his congregation to lie—or at least to remain silent about the truth? How does one teach deception to faithful churchgoers and eager students of Scripture—to people who teach their children by being good examples? A sentence like "extraordinary circumstances call for extraordinary measures" doesn't really help.

"To their own master, servants stand or fall" (Romans 14:4 NIV). What Paul wrote to the Christians in Rome the Chambonnais had internalized in childhood: Everyone stands alone before God. God will judge them. What an individual does or leaves undone is a matter to be resolved within one's conscience. To fall back on the authority of the pastor or the church or the pope is completely out of the question. But where does the formation of one's conscience take place?

In Protestant France at the beginning of the twentieth century, the answer was clear: by reading Scripture. In many homes on the plateau, that specifically meant reading Scripture aloud as a family—daily, sometimes twice daily. This tradition had been passed down uninterrupted from the time of the Reformation. Even though for a long time much of the rural population could not read or write, a Bible lay on the dining table in every Protestant peasant home. Children learned to read from it; indeed, when André was pastor in Le Chambon, the French term *la lecture*, or "reading," still meant "the reading of Scripture."

So what did the Bible have to say about lying? "You shall not lie" sounds as if it were one of the Ten Commandments. But that's not the case. The text actually reads: "You shall not bear false witness against your neighbor" (Exodus 20:16). But what if it was not at all about bearing false witness *against* the neighbor but *for* the neighbor? Was that still a trespass against the law? Or is such reasoning only splitting hairs? People in Le Chambon were suddenly forced to think about such questions.

In Le Chambon, a structure was already in place for such reflection. André's predecessor had established it, and André, with the help of a large notebook, simply guided the process. Every two weeks, André met with thirteen people from the congregation for Bible study. Many of them had been members of the congregation's youth group; some were now serving as leaders of the youth group. These thirteen people were called *les responsables* (the responsible ones), and André led a systematic Bible study course with them.

The first step was to understand the Scripture text and its possible interpretations. Then began the discussion: What might this selection of Scripture mean for the contemporary situation in our congregation and in our society? At the end of each session, André pulled out his large notebook, which contained a list of thirteen districts in and around Le Chambon. Each participant was assigned one of these districts for the next two weeks. There the participant would organize a local discussion group and pass along the insights that *les responsables* had discussed. Many of these "districts" consisted of only a single isolated farmstead.

But now that the church was beginning to organize plans to take in refugees, it was precisely in these places that the Bible studies were especially important. If the peasants, whose farms were hidden deep in the woods, did not go along with the plan, who would give safe haven to the people being persecuted?

The thirteen *responsables* were not sent out to indoctrinate the congregation. The point was not to push the entire congregation in a certain direction or to manipulate them with pious strategies. Given the centuries' worth of highly refined Huguenot stubbornness, such an approach would have been pointless anyway. Originally, the thirteen were sent out because the farmers from the isolated farmsteads were not able to come into the village for Bible study. But now, as the war continued, the point was to engage the Bible in a new way. The members of the church already knew what was in the Bible, in the literal sense; there was no need for anyone to teach them that. But what was the spirit behind the words? Was it possible that one could be true to the letter of Scripture—following exactly what one read—and yet still contradict the spirit of Jesus?

Learning to read all of Scripture through the eyes of Jesus: this was the great task that André wanted to put before the team, along with all the villagers who were reading the Bible. After six years, most of the congregation had already figured out which biblical texts were André's favorites. At the very top was the story of the good Samaritan with its decisive question, who is my neighbor? Then came the Sermon on the Mount, that manifesto of nonresistance. The third text was something of a surprise: a selection from the Old Testament that even some of the most biblically grounded parishioners recalled only vaguely: Numbers 35.

> The Lord spoke to Moses, saying: Speak to the Israelites, and say to them: When you cross the Jordan into the land of Canaan, then you shall select cities to be cities of refuge for you, so that a slayer who kills a person without intent may flee there. The cities shall be for you a refuge from the avenger, so that the slayer may not die until there is a trial before the congregation.
>
> The cities that you designate shall be six cities of refuge for you: you shall designate three cities beyond the Jordan, and three cities in the land of Canaan, to be cities of refuge. These six cities shall serve as refuge for the Israelites, for the resident or transient alien among them, so that anyone who kills a person without intent may flee there. (Numbers 35:9-15)

What did instructions like these, rooted as they were in ancient customs, have to do with Le Chambon in the 1940s? The Jews showing up in the Massif Central mountains seeking protection were not guilty of anything. To the contrary. They were being persecuted simply because they were Jews. There was no other reason. What fascinated André, along with his colleague Edouard Theis, about this passage of Scripture was the idea of a safe haven, a city that existed only to provide asylum. Could Le Chambon become such a city?

There was yet another aspect of this Old Testament idea that both André and Edouard took very seriously and applied to their own situation. In Deuteronomy 19:10, a parallel of this Numbers text, the Israelites were instructed to identify a city of asylum "so that the blood of an innocent person may not be shed in the land that the Lord your God is giving you as an inheritance, thereby bringing bloodguilt upon you." Bloodguilt? Was that not a completely outdated concept? André and Edouard didn't think so.

Whoever offers someone asylum bears the responsibility for whatever happens within that space, even if it is someone else who actually does the harm. If André and Edouard, together with everyone else ready to join in this task, were to make Le Chambon into a city of refuge, then they would have to answer to God for everything that happened there. It was their responsibility not only to do good, but also to prevent evil from happening.

The two pastors decided to write a statement—somewhere between a sermon and a confession of faith—to bring to the congregation. The opportunity presented itself sooner than they would have liked.

***

The Franco-German Armistice at Compiègne was signed on Saturday, June 22, 1940. That same day, Marc Boegner, the church president, gave a radio speech in which he called on the Reformed Church in France to "humbly acknowledge that we have made mistakes that have led our people to the circumstances in which they now find themselves."

André and Edouard took the speech as an occasion to pull together their thoughts in a jointly formulated text and to share it with the congregation at the Sunday service the next day. Boegner was right, they said, but he had not clarified what should be done. Now was not a time when this crucial question could be left up in the air.

In good Huguenot tradition, their speech began with a reference to the children of Israel.

> Just as in Israel's time of great difficulties, the hour of humiliation has now come for us. We want to humble ourselves before God, each of us personally, as leaders of a family or as members of a family, as citizens and Christians, as pastors and presbyters, as

coworkers with the youth, as scouts [*Pfadfinder*], and as ordinary congregational members. We call on God to forgive our guilt, the guilt that we have taken upon ourselves personally and the guilt of our people—the society and the church to which we belong. Only with God's help can we hope to be given new hearts. At the same time, we must guard ourselves against a form of humility that acts as if the disobedient are on the same level as God. Above all else, we want to guard ourselves against confusing abasement, which becomes a kind of disobedience to God. And above all else, we want to guard ourselves against confusing humility with complete discouragement, which gives the impression to those around us that everything is lost.

But wasn't everything basically lost? The congregation looked up. France had not been sufficiently prepared for war. But what would have happened if France had *not* signed the truce and had sent thousands more soldiers to their deaths? Yes, they had been overtaken; but at least that path had not resulted in senseless sacrifices. Marshal Pétain had probably assessed the situation realistically: Germany was and would remain an enormous empire. And France had done well to simply secure a reasonable, somewhat tolerable position in the face of Germany's military superiority. Entering into a compromise made sense.

"It is not true that everything is lost," the two pastors continued in their statement.

The truth of the gospel is not lost; it will continue to be proclaimed from this pulpit and in our discussion groups and home visits. The Word of God is not lost. In it we find all the promises and all the possibilities we need for restoration—for ourselves personally, for our people, and for the church. Our faith is not lost, for true humility does not weaken faith but rather leads to a deeper faith in God and a burning commitment to serve it.

We do not want to use humility as an excuse to renounce freedom, or to become slaves, or to bow before new ideologies like cowards. We must not delude ourselves: in the recent past, totalitarian claims to power have gained enormous respect in the eyes of the world, for this claim, at least from a human perspective, has brought success.

To humble ourselves does not mean to kneel before a false doctrine. We are convinced that the power of this doctrine can be compared to the animal described in Revelation 18—it is nothing other than the antichrist. To state this clearly is, for us, a matter of conscience.

The antichrist. The people in France often spoke of the "enemies of France"—the Jews, the Masons, the Communists, the foreigners, the British—as the ones responsible for the fact that France found itself in this situation. But now the congregation's pastors were speaking of a different enemy.

Dear brothers and sisters, let us above all else let go of every division among us as Christians and all the things that separate us. Let's stop posturing under our distinctive identities and slogans, which are often so full of contempt: right and left; farmer, worker, intellectual; proletariat or owner. Let's stop trying to place the blame on each other. Instead, let each of us extend mutual trust, greeting each other and making each person feel welcome. And like the early Christians, let us remind ourselves whenever we see each other that we are brothers and sisters in Christ.

In the face of all the forces that seek to bend your conscience to their will, the task of the Christian is to resist steadfastly with the weapons of the spirit. To love one another, to forgive, to do good to the enemy—that is our task. But to do this without fleeing from the world, without craven submission, without cowardice. We will resist when our enemies demand from us things that our teachings forbid or that contradict the commands of the gospel.

We will do so without fear, but also without pride or hatred. But this moral resistance will not be possible unless we distance ourselves from a kind of inner slavery that has long ruled us. A time of suffering and deprivation stands before us. All of us have more or less worshiped mammon: the prosperity of our small families, easily accessible pleasures, the ease of life with a bottle in hand. Much is now going to be taken from us. Brothers and sisters, let us learn how to give things up: our pride and egoism, our love of money, our trust in earthly possessions. Let us learn to rely fully on our heavenly Father day by day, to look to him for our daily bread, and to then share it with our brothers and sisters, whom we should love as we love ourselves.

May God free us from our sorrows just as much as he frees us from our false security. May he give us, his children, a peace that no one can take away. May he comfort us in our sadness and in our temptations and consider us worthy members of the church of Jesus Christ, the body of Christ, in the expectation of his kingdom of justice and love, in which his will is done, on earth as it is in heaven.

Was that a sermon? Should the response be "Amen"? Some people in the congregation that Sunday morning murmured something like an amen and added a small sigh.

Did that mean that they had now made a commitment?

PART V

18

A Village on a Hill

Le Chambon, 1939–40

E ven in an era without email or Twitter, small details in distant settings could be linked through an astonishing set of connections. Approximately one thousand kilometers (over six hundred miles) from Le Chambon was a little village in Germany by the name of Ranstadt. It was accessible from Frankfurt only by driving through the Wetterau Valley in the direction of the Vogelsberg, then turning off the autobahn onto a series of local roads. In the 1930s the village had a very overqualified pastor. This was the first parallel to Le Chambon. Peter Brunner, nearly one year to the day older than André Trocmé, had studied in Marburg, then at Harvard University, and then, like André, at the Sorbonne. Already as a thirty-three-year-old he had accepted a position at the University of Giessen as a theology professor. He was a sort of Lutheran shooting star—a conservative who had no fears or vices.

In this context—and because he harbored the hope of still being able to disrupt the emergence of a National Socialist regime—Brunner had established an antifascist political party—and promptly lost his professorship. After all, it was 1933. He was then transferred to Ranstadt, a place as far from being a city as Chicago is from being a village. There he joined the Pastors' Emergency League, a council of pastors that objected to Nazism and that Martin Niemöller, the well-known anti-Nazi pastor, had founded.

Through his stirring sermons, Brunner brought the members of his traditional and previously disinterested congregation to the place where they were ready to join the Confessing Church, a movement within German Protestantism that was opposed to Nazi efforts. Brunner's fearless public behavior led to a bitter conflict between the village mayor and the congregation, one that ended only when Brunner was detained by the secret police and sent to Dachau.

When Brunner returned three months later, he was missing all his teeth, and it was clear that he was suffering from an odd nervous condition. But he refused to tell anyone what he had experienced. He had also been forced to sign a statement that he would no longer appear in public.

***

Only one friend of Brunner's seemed to have known more than all the others. Otto Salomon was a Jew from Frankfurt who had been baptized as a young man and who wrote articles and books. In 1935, German authorities ordered him to cease all publications. Salomon first assumed the Dutch-sounding pseudonym Johan Maarten, but later a pseudonym that sounded very Christian—Otto Bruder—and he wrote an account of the pastor from Ranstadt. The title of his little book sounded harmless, but those who knew Scripture well already had a clear hint about its content: *The Village on the Hill.* The title harkened back to the Sermon on the Mount: "A city built on a hill cannot be hid" (Matthew 5:14). The idea that whatever happened in the city would one day come to light was exactly what Otto Salomon wanted. Sooner or later, what was happening in Ranstadt would become widely known.

"I am a simple woodcutter and I cannot speak eloquently because I never attended high school," wrote Salomon. "But I want to recount everything exactly as it happened with our pastor Stefan Grund, who was sent to prison two months ago." So began the account of the alleged woodcutter. None of the changes in the names or circumstances could prevent the book from censorship in Germany, however. In 1938, Salomon seized the opportunity to escape into Switzerland, and in 1939 his book appeared with the help of a Zürich publisher. That same year, the book was translated into French and not long thereafter came into the hands of Charles Guillon, the mayor of Le Chambon.

Guillon was a pious man who was deeply influenced by the YMCA and who was active in the organization's international movement. When he read the book by "Johan Maarten," it was as if someone had given him a pair of glasses made with a prescription just for him. The text moved him profoundly. He promptly ordered a whole box of the books and began to pass them out to everyone he met.

Was not Le Chambon, in the truest sense of the term, a "village on the hill"? Could those things that happened there be revealed one day not only to the eyes of God but also to the eyes of the whole world? The village described in the book had an upright mayor who resigned directly after the Nazis came to power. The subsequent mayor was a thoroughgoing Nazi and played a key role in the arrest of the pastor. What kind of a mayor would he, Guillon, be if the political situation in France became more tense?

After reading the book, Guillon had a very clear vision: he wanted to be a mayor who could open the eyes of his villagers and prepare them for the great task ahead. He wanted to make it clear to them what sort of responsibility the village and all its inhabitants would soon need to bear.

Then came June 22, 1940, the day that the Franco-German Armistice was signed and that Marshal Philippe Pétain essentially took charge over every mayor, even in the Vichy Free Zone. André Trocmé and Edouard Theis gave their joint sermon the next day, June 23. On that same evening, Charles Guillon resigned his office, as had the courageous mayor in the book he'd read. Guillon had wanted to be a responsible mayor, but that plainly would not be possible under this regime. If he wanted to make a difference, he would need to express his resistance in some other way.

That much became clear to him on the evening of June 23. Soon thereafter, Guillon moved to Valence, a town about seventy kilometers (roughly forty miles) from Le Chambon where the YMCA had an office. What he was going to do there was not at all clear to the Chambonnais—at least not initially.

***

The new Vichy government was barely in office two weeks before it took its first action against the Jews. Jews who had become naturalized citizens were abruptly deprived of their French citizenship. Anti-Jewish placards set the tone. Propaganda films depicted young Frenchmen atop hay wagons at harvesttime, shirts off, engaged in honest work, while "the Jews" gambled at casinos or lounged on the beaches of Côte d'Azur. Then, in October, the private anti-Semitism of individual citizens became an official obligation. Inspired by the Nuremberg Laws, Pétain issued laws that forced Jews out of all government offices and many other professions as well. Traditional French principles of *Lib egalité, fraternité* (liberty, equality, fraternity) were set aside. Now the slogan was *Travail, famille, patrie* (Work, family, fatherland), in which it was clear that Jews had no rights whatsoever in the fatherland. Who could have imagined that France would need so little encouragement from the German Reich in carrying out these policies? Events unfolded—many of them initiated by the French Waffen SS and not even ordered by Germany—with a kind of preemptive obedience. Posters on the walls of houses announced: "Under this symbol [i.e., the Waffen SS], you and your European comrades will be victorious!" Collaboration, under the Vichy regime, was not a negative term but a slogan: If we work together with our mighty neighbor without any hesitation, we will soon be standing on the side of the victor!

After some initial hesitance, Pétain, sometimes known as the "hero of Verdun," became a good student of his much younger teacher, Adolf Hitler, in promoting a leadership cult. Now that the French Third Republic was buried by the Vichy regime, it was an easy matter to do away with "La Marseillaise," the patriotic hymn of the French Revolution. The new hymn was called "Maréchal, nous voilà!" ("Marshal [Pétain], Here We Are!"). As a blaring fanfare, the masses sang, "All your children love you. You give your life to save the fatherland for a second time."

Who didn't want to follow a führer who was opposed to continuing the war? Who didn't want to be rational and position themselves on the side of the future victor?

The people in Chambon didn't want to. Nor did the people in Tence, in Fay-sur-Lignon, Mazet-Saint-Voy, Devesset, Saint-Agrève, Mars, Freycenet-Saint-Jeures, Araules . . . These were tiny places, sometimes only two or three neighboring farmsteads that quietly began to resist the new regime. Not officially or politically, with arguments or demonstrations, but in practical ways. Le

Chambon took the lead, but a whole network of resistance was developing on the plateau.

***

Apart from the resignation of the mayor, the period of resistance began with as little fanfare as Magda's search for a new pair of shoes. Since October 4, 1940, a law on "Aliens of Jewish Race" had declared: "Citizens of the Jewish race can be forced to move from their home at any time to a place determined by the state. By the proclamation, residents of the Jewish race who have foreign citizenship can be interned in a special camp upon the decision of the prefect of the department."

Suddenly, Jews throughout the whole country were in transit, all of them trying to preempt their forced relocation. They had already lost their livelihoods. Now, finding themselves abruptly without work, dispossessed, and regarded as enemies, they searched in despair for safe places to stay. Along with the French Jews came refugees from Germany, Austria, and Poland, and more came daily. To make matters worse, residence permits were no longer being issued to non-Jewish foreigners. Where were they to go?

For the Vichy government, the solution was obvious: the internment camps from World War I were still available. In recent years, some of these camps had already been reactivated for the refugees of the Spanish Civil War. Now Jews and others who were not welcome as citizens of France could go there. And in the end, they were forced to.

Gurs, located at the foot of the Pyrenees, was one such camp, as were the barracks of Le Vernet by Perpignan. Directly adjacent to it, Rivesaltes was prepared as a supplemental camp, as was Les Milles, close to Aix-en-Provence. Designating these sites as "camps," as they were called in French, sounded much better than "concentration camps." But there was not much difference between the two. The French camps were not extermination death camps, but they were sites secured by concertina wire and governed by the realities of hunger, cold, and daily humiliation, all of which led to the deaths of many interned there. Initially, the operation of the camps was overseen exclusively by the French rather than their German allies. By the time Germans took control, three thousand people had already died.

Did the average French citizen know about the existence of these camps or anything about the conditions in them? People in Le Chambon knew. As in Germany, those who wished to know about the camps could do so, even if all the details weren't published in the newspapers.

Resistance initially meant protecting people from being sent to one of the camps—first by providing shelter, and then by helping them disappear. Avoiding attention from the authorities was paramount. Could there have been a place better suited for this than the high plateau at the end of the world?

***

The first refugees to come to Le Chambon were people from large cities, often Paris—well-educated intellectuals who had, until very recently, practiced professions and moved in dignified circles. The first people to receive these refugees were the strictly religious Darbyite farmers. Carrying the few possessions that they could manage to bring with them, the new arrivals found themselves standing in a farmyard in a forest of fir trees somewhere outside Le Chambon. At first glance, the homes may have made a great impression, but on closer inspection, the refugees would have seen that the home and barn were one and the same building. The warmth of the cows and sheep could also heat the living room. The farmers found this to be practical; the Parisians regarded it as outrageous and simply appalling. The stench penetrated every tiny crack.

And what were the refugees supposed to do during the long days? The farmers thought it was clear: roll up their sleeves and plunge into the farmwork. But the farmers held this thought only for a week or so. They soon realized that these city folk were of very little use—at least not for the tasks that they were facing. The newcomers started to name the chickens—names that came from French literature, such as characters in Racine's tragedies. Thus, chickens around Le Chambon became known as Iphigénie, Clytemnestre, Andromaque, and Bérénice. Only the pigs did not become godchildren with classical monikers: they were all simply named Adolf.

The refugees themselves bore names like Benjamin, Levi, Judith, and Esther—the very same names the farmers' children had been given. For generations the Huguenots had given their children biblical first names, especially names from the Old Testament, as a conscious way of distinguishing themselves from the Catholics. Those who had become Darbyites also maintained this tradition. And now the tradition proved to have an extremely practical consequence. If the authorities came to the farm, who could say if little Eli was a farmer's child or the offspring of a Jewish refugee? (Provided he was not old enough to divulge his family name.)

The refugee's family names had to be altered. Cohen, for example, became Colin, and people set about to create new last names that began with the same letter. After all, in the end one could not know whether the engraved initial on a penholder or the embroidery on a napkin might one day come to have tragic or lifesaving consequences.

Now the only things lacking were new identity papers for the slightly altered names. The thought that they needed to muster a sort of criminal energy for this task weighed heavily on the hearts of the farmers.

But they braced themselves in the same way they always did: with devotions at the beginning and end of the day.

19

Every Child We Can Save

Le Chambon, 1940–41

O nce a stone is thrown into the water, there is no way to prevent ripples. The resistance had begun. Now, inexorably, one consequence followed another.

When people live in hiding, they need something to eat, but they can do nothing to earn it. Nor do they receive ration cards from the government. The necessary cards must somehow be procured.

When people need to be given new names, counterfeit papers must be professionally prepared; amateur work could have deadly consequences. That means that the paper, stamps, and signatures must be exactly right.

When people align themselves against the state, they must be able to live with the reality of being identified as criminals. Those who want to live as lifelong irreproachable citizens are in the wrong place.

Whoever assumes a task of this magnitude must find allies. Who might be sympathetic? Who is trustworthy? Who has the necessary connections—perhaps international connections—or technical know-how or financial resources that could be tapped? Magda and others discerned these networks in the village and, indeed, on the entire plateau.

André was consumed by very different concerns. In late 1940 he traveled to Marseille. The city on the Mediterranean Sea was quickly becoming a center for relief organizations. But André made the trip not to seek support for Le Chambon but to volunteer himself in support of the work. He had discussed this with his presbytery. André met with Burns Chalmers, a leading Quaker from the United States, to explore where his service could be of use in one of the camps in southern France. The Quakers had started working with interned refugees through the American Friends Service Committee.

"Don't go to one of the camps," Chalmers told him directly. "There are already too many do-gooders bustling about there, and they are not making the situation any easier. But tell me—don't you come from one of the mountain villages? And wouldn't that perhaps be a very secure location?"

"Yes, at least compared to some places," said André. "That's why so many different people have already sought us out."

Chalmers continued, "Our problem at the moment is this: We are working together with doctors and are trying to procure as many medical certificates as we can for people in the camps, declaring that they are unfit to work. These people supposedly are going to be sent into forced labor in Germany. If we are not able in this way to save the father, then we do all we can to get a certificate for the mother. If, despite our efforts, both parents are deported, then we focus our attention on the children. And that's where we bump up against our limits. Every child we can save from the camps needs a place of refuge outside the camps. Yet what French community is ready to take this problem on themselves?

Chalmers looked André straight in the eyes. Then he posed a question that both gave André's trip a new purpose and brought it to an end: "Is your village prepared to become the place of refuge that we need?"

André heard a heavy stone splashing into the water. And he imagined the circles it would create!

"The children: there are, no doubt, many, many of them. All of them will need to be housed and fed. And they'll all need to go to school," André said slowly and reflectively, while the next questions were already emerging in his mind.

"Find the necessary houses and caretakers; we'll take care of the finances," said Chalmers simply and clearly.

When André returned to Le Chambon, the congregation was happy and surprised—his absence turned out to only be a short excursion. They already had their pastor back! What they didn't fully realize was that they also, indirectly, had their mayor back as well. Indeed, it was Charles Guillon who would serve as the middleman who ensured that the promised financial support would arrive securely at those places he knew so well.

***

The stone created circles whose magnitude André could never have imagined. It did not take long before Le Chambon found itself in the middle of hurried activities. There were the Quakers, as had been agreed upon in Marseille; then came Secours Suisse, which belonged to the Swiss Red Cross; CIMADE, a Protestant organization led by two French women who had started visiting people interned in the camps even before the start of the Vichy regime; OSE, a French Jewish group that focused especially on children; and of course, the YMCA, which had long had a foothold in the community through the village's former mayor, Guillon. All of these organizations had heard of the wonderful possibilities emerging on the plateau.

And all the groups met with a positive surprise: Le Chambon may have been a little backwater town, but it had a train station! In 1902, a station was supposed to be built in nearby Le Mazet, which would have spared the rail line a few meters of elevation. But the Darbyites who lived there were not interested in having such a modern tool of the devil coming to their village, so the train line was forced to go farther up the mountain. The train station eventually bore the double name of Le Chambon-Mazet. The presence of a train station meant that the organizations were spared the complications of hiring cars and drivers; it was only necessary to accompany the children in the train.

Nonetheless, there were still innumerable details that needed to be clarified and arranged. How dangerous was it to transport and provide shelter to Jewish children? Would a discharge permit from one of the camps be taken seriously by the authorities, or would the whole operation have to take place secretly? Most of the children had been born outside the country and were not French citizens. Thus, they were children who officially did not exist and for whom the state had not provided teachers, class-rooms, or books. The children would therefore need to be sent to school "without papers." Alternatively, they would need identity papers with French birthplaces, in which case they would need to speak at least passable French.

Questions piled onto questions. Where did people discuss all these details, making and scraping plans, scribbling names on lists, exchanging money in envelopes? In the parsonage, natu-rally. Many of the conversations and plans were made right in Magda's kitchen.

André Trocmé telling the refugee children a story in Le Chambon.
Private collection.

But these activities were also happening in many other kitchens throughout the village. The first reason for this was simple:
kitchens were the only heated room in the house. The second
reason was strategic: at no time should it appear as if these secret
activities were being organized centrally.

During these weeks, every free spot, including André's workroom, became an emergency dorm. A father and his nearly adult
son camped on the sofa now beside André's desk. Like all guests
in the parsonage, they were only to be housed there in passing.
But then it was one or two nights more, and one or two nights
more . . .

The activities in the parsonage never had a conspiratorial feel
to them. That simply was not the mood of the house. Things happened noisily and with good humor—"like a happy beehive," one
of the refugees later recalled. Of course there were also frustrations, misunderstandings, and accidents. Under steadily growing

pressure, neither the guests nor the hosts suddenly became saints. Helpers were occasionally overstressed and on edge, and the refugees in their care could also be irritable and capricious.

***

Among those people who more or less lived in the parsonage was Simone, a woman from the town of Maubeuge, where the Trocmé family had lived before coming to Le Chambon. Her husband was a soldier fighting against the Germans. As long as he was gone, Simone wanted to remain with the Trocmé family. She had lived with them before and after Nelly's birth, and she liked helping the family.

One day she received a letter containing a newspaper clipping with the obituary of her husband. Simone's despair was immense. But she remained in Le Chambon. Now she wanted to do something that had a larger purpose. Through wind and storm, she continued to visit scattered farms throughout the plateau searching for shelter for new refugee families.

One day she received news of the pending arrival of a family from Paris. Simone soon found a suitable farm situated in a high, remote location close to a mill. It was cold, and a penetrating rain was falling steadily from the gray skies.

"I ran to the train station in order to welcome the wife and her son," Magda recalled.

The father was supposed to arrive later. I explained very clearly to both of them how to find the farm and the precautions that they should take. But then the woman suddenly became excited and exclaimed: "But Madame Trocmé, you are not assuming that I am going to go out by foot in this rain!" "Oh, madame," I replied. "Yes, it is raining, and my friend Simone has been running through the mountains all night long in order to find shelter for you. And those of us who are bending over backward to help people like you . . . did you think that we do this only when the weather is pleasant?"

Magda reflected,

Life was complicated. The children were hungry; we were hungry; the counterfeit papers that were being created in a secret hideaway all took time. And it always took forever for the ration cards for food to arrive. I ate almost nothing and became as thin as a nail in the wall. I simply had too many responsibilities on my shoulders. To find food I first needed to free up some time. Before or after school, I would jump on my bicycle and ride to various farmers. There were also ration cards for cigarettes and alcohol. So I would trade cigarette rations for firewood and potatoes. I ripped up the alcohol ration cards. They would have been especially valuable, but we belonged to the Blue Cross, and André could have never endured the thought of me passing out wine rations to people who were already strongly predisposed to alcoholism. I can recall a large load of firewood that we were supposed to receive. But then the man said, "Only if you give me your wine ration cards." Everyone's nerves were frayed, even those of us in the parsonage.

Until now the focus had been on meeting the needs of individual guests and refugee families. This was difficult enough, since rarely was it a question of housing them for only a single night. Often new quarters needed to be found for reasons of security. Sometimes new accommodations had to be found because of an incompatibility in character or personality between the newcomer and the host; in other cases, it was so as not to impose on the host for an unreasonable length of time. New guests arrived every day. These included young guests in every train car who were mixed in alongside the ordinary passengers.

The youngest unaccompanied refugees were four years old; the oldest were nearly adults. The younger children had no idea what was happening to them or why their parents had remained behind in the camps. The older ones knew very well. Some of them had experienced deportation along with their parents, and for many, this was not the first time they had been forcibly separated from grandparents or siblings, uncles and aunts.

For nearly all of them, the trip on the small train up to Le Chambon was only one more leg of a long, traumatic journey. A hasty departure; a journey without knowing where you were headed; being entrusted to people you didn't know, and who were exactly as helpless and wounded as you. The thought that these children could be thankful to be sitting in this train sounds almost cynical. Yet it was indeed their good fortune. And the women who traveled with them knew: if their charges had not come aboard this laboring, gasping little locomotive, then all of them would now be crowded together on a big train heading east.

***

As in all the occupied lands, the train companies fulfilled their obligations. If the Germans wanted long trains to run from southern France to Poland, then the French train system organized that efficiently. Pierre-Eugène Fournier, the head of the French railway, was an enthusiastic supporter of Marshal Pétain, and therefore French collaboration in all matters related to rail travel went forward without a hitch. Train schedules were rearranged to give priority to deportation. Trains, along with their crews, were on standby so that Jews could be "delivered" as forced laborers whenever an employer wished. And because Fournier was so dependable, it was even left to him to determine who qualified as a Jew. French and German laws may have occasionally had a somewhat different perspective on this question, but the Vichy regime trusted Fournier to make the right call in any questionable circumstance.

And yet, one train after another arrived at the plateau. Beginning in the spring of 1941, small children and teenagers—Polish, German, Austrian, Dutch, and Czech schoolchildren alike—filled the homes of Le Chambon. New housing was arranged; bed-and-breakfast establishments were repurposed. A sudden wave of city children, all badly in need of recreation and fresh air, arrived. Le Chambon's function as a summer resort for children from the surrounding areas served the village well. Obviously, children in need of fresh air required places to stay. At least that was the story.

A group of Jewish children who were sheltered by the residents of Le Chambon. Chambon Foundation.

Vichy France at that time was "only" collaborating; it had not yet been occupied. In the air battles above England, the German army had experienced its first defeats, but on the Eastern Front it was marching from victory to victory, and no one knew when Germany would also lay claim to the rest of France, including Le Chambon.

Individual children were distributed across the plateau to live with families and attend school in the tiny villages. The larger groups remained in Le Chambon and lived in the hotel, Tante Soly, in the town center, or in the newly opened guesthouse, La Guespy, closer to the edge of town. The children attended the elementary school; the older ones, or those who were particularly gifted, went to the École Cévenole.

***

There in the schoolyard of École Cévenole, the flag of the new French state awaited the new students. They needed to salute the flag every morning; in every classroom, there was a picture of Marshal Pétain. According to a new ordinance, both needed to be visible.

Could one expect these children to salute the flag that represented the state which had torn their families apart and sent their parents off to their likely deaths? André and Edouard decided that neither the new children nor the local students could—or should—be expected to do so. They could not speak for the public schools, but in their own school they emphatically wanted to avoid any expression of allegiance to the new regime.

Eventually, they found a solution. Surprisingly enough, the solution emerged thanks to the help of the village schoolmaster, Roger Darcissac—the same man whose perspective André had thought to be so limited during his first months in Le Chambon.

"I have an idea," Darcissac proposed one day. "We will set up our flagpole close to the wall, there where the schoolyard borders the street. My students will stand in a half circle in the direction of the wall and salute the flag. You can arrange your students on the sidewalk and form the other half of the circle. They can see and salute the flag above the wall. Then they can go into their classrooms on the other side of the street."

And indeed, every morning for several weeks, a few students from École Cévenole gathered near a village schoolteacher, who regarded Pétain as the savior of the fatherland, and saluted the flag. But then the half circle began to dwindle in size, until finally it was decided that a weekly salute of the flag by the students of École Cévenole would probably suffice. Not long thereafter, the distasteful ritual was dropped. It remained to be seen how long this could go on unnoticed and unpunished.

***

An opportunity to test the limits of the small liberties one could take in a village came for a second time that summer. (Of course, by sheltering "illegal children," the village was taking large liberties as well, but those were happening in secret.) August 1 had been proclaimed as a new national holiday. In honor of the military, all church bells were supposed to ring for fifteen minutes starting at twelve noon.

André showed the government order to the church custodian. "You should, of course, simply do nothing, Amélie," he said. "Even if someone tries to force you to ring the bell."

Amélie nodded. The small woman, who could have easily been launched into the air by the bell rope as she pulled on it, was a Darbyite. Like many of her fellow believers, she avoided all unnecessary speech, especially when she was in the presence of a man.

On August 1, the townspeople of Le Chambon heard the loud pealing of the bells from the tower of the Catholic church, lasting exactly fifteen minutes. The bell tower of the Protestant church, however, remained silent.

The next day, André met Amélie in the village. "So, Amélie," he said. "Did everything go all right, or did you have a problem?"

"Everything went fine. No problem."

"Did anyone come to the church?" André probed.

"Yes," Amélie answered. "There were two women. Women from the summer cottages wearing lots of makeup."

"And?"

"They wanted me to ring the bells. 'It's a national holiday! The marshal ordered the ringing of the bells!'"

"And what did you say?"

"I said, 'The bells do not belong to the marshal; they belong to God. We ring them for God or not at all.'"

André beamed. "Bravo! And then?"

"Then the women wanted me to open the church so that they could ring the bells themselves," Amélie said. "But I defended my temple! I stood there just like this!" And then the small, gentle Amélie demonstrated how she had stood, arms outstretched, her back against the church door, in front of the women.

My temple? André had to chuckle. Amélie was not even a member of the congregation. She had merely sought out some part-time work and had taken on the custodian job for a few hours a week. But yesterday her part-time job had transformed her into a sentry in the battle between church and state.

Cheerfully, the two parted ways. There was little doubt that the Darbyites would continue to preach that Christians were not permitted to take part in political affairs, since one's faith had nothing to do with the things of this world. But there was also no doubt in André's mind that he could count on Amélie in the future.

20

"You Need to Be Careful"

Le Chambon, 1942

There were three telephones in Le Chambon. Dialing 1 would connect you with the mayor (after the departure of Charles Guillon, a new man who was loyal to the regime occupied the office). Dialing 2 reached the town physician, Dr. Le Forestier. Dialing 3 connected the caller with the hotel at the town's only intersection.

The parsonage did not need a telephone, because there were the four children. Magda sent her own scouts in every imaginable direction on errands for the cause. But she also did not hesitate to grab a child by the sleeve in the middle of the village and give him or her an assignment: "Run quickly to Madame Barraud and tell her that everything is set up for this evening." And then the child would run and pass along the message: "Everything is set up for this evening."

It was crucial that the villagers could depend on each other, and the children were no exception. To this end, they developed their own code. In Darbyite families, the phrase "We still have three Old Testaments at home" meant "three Jews are living with us." The villagers quickly learned not to ask in which home or on what farm people were hiding, as the fewer people had information, the better. The only relevant question was which homes were not harboring anyone, since those could be considered as potential spots for newcomers. There were not many homes or farms left in that category.

All of this required discipline and imagination. Trapdoors were built. False walls were constructed. One farmer hid falsified documents in a beehive, another in his mother's mausoleum.

To preserve appearances, Jewish children—who were now Christian, according to their official papers—celebrated all the Christian holidays, including Carnival, for which Edouard Theis dug out shawls and head coverings from his missionary years in Madagascar. But in order not to alienate the children from their own traditions, the villagers helped their guests observe Jewish holy days—secretly, of course.

Le Chambon was busy, and with it the entire plateau. The normally leisurely rhythms of country life were transformed into the energetic swarming of an anthill. And Magda—the woman the American doctor had recommended three hours' rest on a chaise longue every day—this Magda was in the thick of it. She was always on the go, crisscrossing the village to the scattered classrooms, uphill and down on the bicycle, up and down the stairs in the parsonage. She was busy without pause, often tired to the point of falling over. But Magda had no doubts whatsoever that in these moments she was doing what was important or that it was exactly the right thing to do.

André and Magda Trocmé in Le Chambon. Chambon Foundation.

"And we were indeed happy," wrote André many years later.

For the first and last time in our lives we were truly happy during those years in Le Chambon, despite the war. The slender, somewhat feverish young girl of earlier years had blossomed into a beautiful, vigorous plant. I thought she had become more than pretty: classic, beautiful, strong, and always full of fire. The photos from that time, that show her standing among her four children, make this beauty clear. A lady from the congregation once said something to me that I've never forgotten: "Your wife possesses three qualities that are only rarely found in one and the same person: beauty, intelligence, and kindness." And that's exactly right. Magda carried with her the beauty of Florence. Sometimes she would give a glance in which her eyes flashed with indignation; sometimes she looked on with complete concern and tenderness for her loved ones. And it was fitting that she always spoke loudly in her rough Italian voice. Sometimes what she said had been carefully thought out; sometimes she spoke with passion; sometimes with humor—but it was always original. In any case, whenever she spoke, the old parsonage vibrated so that neither her children nor her husband nor anyone else was ever bored. She was never freed from a certain agitation, above all in regard to little things—a sort of constant concern for details, an anxious vexation, under which we all suffered but which always seemed to accompany her. Nevertheless, I happily endured the burden of this constant unrest for the privilege of living alongside such a generous, intelligent, energetic, and selfless woman.

I often returned to the house in the dark after a meeting or a visit. I needed to take care not to lose my way, since the blowing wind quickly covered my tracks in the snow. I was only fully at peace when I could hear the rushing waters of the Lignon, which helped to orient me in the right direction. I stumbled along through the snow, until out of the fog I could see a brightly lit window frame. Then I knew that I had made it, and the last steps through the village were only a prelude to my arrival in the large entryway of the parsonage, where I would knock the snow off my shoes. Then I stood in the dining room, embraced by eight arms: "Papa, Papa!" Jacot [Jacques] and Daniel each held on tightly to one of my legs and stood on my feet so that I could walk with them "like an elephant." Jean-Pierre wrapped himself around my waist and stuck his "mop head" under my arm. Nelly choked me with her arms around my neck, but I still had one hand free to stroke her beautiful silklike hair and to pull a little on her blond braids. Maman remained standing at the spot where, until that moment, she had been busy, and observed the overwhelming spectacle. And I, who earlier in life had been such a lonely human being, I was like a tree full of branches and fruit. Quite simply, I was happy.

The parsonage idyll. The suffering of children whose parents were being deported. The relief of families who had escaped a security sweep. All of these realities were happening at the same time. The fate of one person played out only a few steps from the door of another person. Of course, living together so intensely brought mixed emotions. Stories were passed along from farmyard to farmyard—sometimes sad, sometimes funny—but stories that were, above all, intended to comfort. Here someone did indeed make it. There two people had found each other after all. Here a letter had arrived.

***

In the summer of 1942, however, a story was making the rounds that left little room for hope, a story that quickly proved to be a horrific fact. In Paris, all the Jews were driven together into a sports stadium close to the Eiffel Tower—the Vélodrome d'Hiver (Vel' d'Hiv), which served as a racetrack for cyclists during the winter. For five days the Jews were held there, in the middle of July, without food, without water, without beds, without any wash facilities, and with toilets that soon began to overflow. The Gestapo and the French police had coordinated their efforts perfectly, and now at least a thousand men, three thousand women, and more than four thousand children suffered in the brutal heat under a glass roof that had been painted dark blue to confuse enemy planes.

Operation Spring Breeze was the cynical name for this operation. Until that point, policies in Vichy France had often been worse than the actions in the occupied zone, but now the policies affected every Jew, without exception, who had not already fled Paris or the suburbs around it. Until the occupation, the majority of French Jews had lived in or near Paris. During the first wave of arrests, it was mostly the men who had been taken, which is why those in the stadium were mostly women, children, and elderly men.

In the meantime, it was known in Le Chambon that internment camps had been prepared also in the north, among them the infamous camp Drancy, northeast of Paris. From there the trains traveled directly to Poland. Soon the news came on the BBC: those who had survived the days in the Vel' d'Hiv were now being loaded into trains. Many of them had already died in the stadium, and some had committed suicide. Those who tried to flee had been shot on the spot.

By now it was clear to André that it was not only valiant Protestant individuals who needed to demonstrate civil courage; now it was time for the Reformed Church of France to unite in protest over the treatment of the Jews. In a letter to the chief rabbi of France, Marc Boegner, the Reformed Church president, had already expressed his regret for the events that had taken place, and he had met repeatedly with Marshal Pétain, the chief of state of Vichy, France, as well as with Pierre Laval, the Vichy head of government, to plead for moderation: "Please use your influence to ensure that no Jewish children under the age of sixteen will be deported," Boegner wrote. Pétain, in turn, made him a member of the national council. A diplomat like Boegner, who could politely point out injustices with silk-gloved hands, belonged in the ranks of the most important men in Vichy. That, at least, is how André saw it. At the Reformed Church synod, not long after the raid that led to Vel' d'Hiv, things came to a head.

"The church hesitates and contradicts itself," André accused Boegner, "since every congregation responds differently, depending on the pastor and the local situation. What we need is a clear message to all Protestants: Protect the Jews!"

"That's completely crazy!" Boegner responded, equally agitated. "You will invite the rage of all of Hitler's Germany to the Reformed Church of France, to this little flock that has been entrusted to me. The foremost issue at the moment is the physical survival of Protestantism in France. That's what I'm going to focus on."

"I was incensed," André wrote later. "I felt I had been conned by Boegner. And I was ashamed of the Reformed Church of France."

***

As luck would have it, that summer the authorities announced that Le Chambon would receive an eminent visitor. Georges Lamirand, the Vichy government's minister of youth, wished to pay a visit in person. "Give this visit the ceremonial character that it deserves," read the announcement, which was addressed not to the mayor but to André, the pastor and founder of the École Cévenole.

"Theis and I were filled with panic," André recalled.

From the very beginning, Vichy had attempted to bring together all youth organizations under the so-called Blue Shirts of the "Compagnons de France." For two years we had done everything in our power to protect our children from the grip of the state.

With their fascist flag salute, their bugle calls, marches, social events, work camps, and their cult of the fatherland and of Marshal Pétain, they were actually too similar to the Hitler Youth to have much success in France. The Catholic and Protestant scouts had also immediately insisted on their independence. The state had contributed little, but now it was a generous financial supporter of the youth movement in order to control them effectively.

André and Edouard Theis tried to decline the visit. But this honor was not so easily evaded, and it seemed as if everything had already been organized from above. There was to be a banquet, a parade to the athletic field for a youth gathering, a reception at the Protestant church—and a worship service!

There was no way to avoid it. The only thing André and Edouard could influence in some small way was the menu. So they decided that the food served at the banquet for the dignitaries would be exactly what ordinary people were able to buy with their ration cards, nothing more.

The events took their course, and on August 15, 1942, André found himself playing the role of the cheerful conversationalist as the host of the table where the minister of youth was seated. If he was going to be forced into this honorable position, then he at least wanted to be able to steer the conversation. As André and Edouard had planned, instead of a lavish meal, the guests were served plates with meager portions. Lamirand smiled. "This is even better," he said with an air of generous renunciation. "It is more in keeping with the spirit of Marshal Pétain, and it's more patriotic."

After the meal, André climbed into Lamirand's car, which was supposed to lead the official parade. The car, however, drove alone on empty streets. Not a single person stood on the sidewalks;

there were no flags in the windows. Lamirand politely cleared his throat.

At the athletic field of the school came yet another surprise. Clearly, no one had prepared a formal youth gathering. Instead, hundreds of curious children crowded around the minister and tried their hardest to shake his hand: "Bonjour, m'sieur!"

"Bonjour, bonjour!" he answered, expressing his pleasure at the "spontaneity" of his little fans. What else could he do? The speech he had prepared remained in his pocket. The setting was not right for it.

At the church, Edouard and André had refused to preach to a delegation from the state. So a Swiss colleague assumed that task. But even this had a comic quality to it: a Swiss pastor, of all people, promising allegiance to the French government—as long as it did not contradict God's law and the laws of the state. Lamirand turned around in his pew as André gave him a song-book and encouraged him to sing.

After the service ended, a group of young people were waiting for the minister in front of the church door. They were student from the upper grades of the École Cévenole.

"Monsieur le Ministre, we have written a paper. Please read it—now!" Lamirand paused and took the paper in his hand.

"We have heard of the horrible events that took place in Paris three weeks ago," it read.

We know from experience that these things taking place in the occupied zone may soon be happening in the unoccupied zone as well, even if it is presented as a spontaneous idea of the French administrators. We fear that the mass deportation of the Jews may soon commence here in the south as well. For these reasons, we think it important to inform you that there are Jews living here among us. However, we do not make any distinction between Jews and non-Jews, since that would go against the teachings of the gospel. If our school friends, whose only mistake is that they happened to be born in another place, receive an order to be deported or even just to be counted and identified, we will encourage them to refuse to obey that order, and we intend to hide them in the best ways possible.

Lamirand turned pale. "These questions have nothing to do with me," he said curtly. "Take them to the provincial government." And with a few quick steps he reached his car.

The provincial governor, a Mr. Bach, remained standing at the church door as the minister's car drove off. Furious, he turned to André. "Monsieur le Pasteur," he said, stretching himself upright. "This day was supposed to be a day of national unity. But you are sowing seeds of disunity!"

"What exactly does national unity look like if our brothers are threatened with deportation?" André answered.

"It's true that I have already received the order, and I intend to carry it out," said the governor. "Foreign Jews who live in our territory are not your brothers. They belong neither to your church nor to your fatherland. And in any case, this has nothing to do with deportation."

"What then?"

"What I know comes from Marshal Pétain himself," the governor replied. "And he does not lie. Our great leader is an intelligent man. Just as the British established a Zionist homeland for Jews in Palestine, all the Jews in Europe are going to be gathered in Poland. There they will receive land and houses, and they can lead their lives in a way appropriate for them instead of infecting the West with their ways. In a few days our people are going to come to Le Chambon to do a census of the Jews here."

"We don't know what a Jew is," André said. "We only know human beings."

Now the two men were standing across from each other, their faces bright red. This exchange could not be without consequences. And it was clear who had the longer end of the stick.

"Monsieur Trocmé," said Bach in a sharp, threatening tone, "you need to be careful. Seven of your fellow citizens are writing regular reports about the subversive activities that are taking place here—under your watch. Until now I have not given any weight to these letters, but I'm being updated. If you are not careful, it's going to be you who is arrested. I think we're clear now. Goodbye!"

21

Arrest and the Village's Farewell

Le Chambon, 1943

André knew that matters were coming to a head. Nearly a half a year had passed since the threat from the provincial government. He had been left in peace for longer than might have been expected. André had written his will long ago, on the same day the French army capitulated before the advance of the Germans. In the will, he had clearly articulated the reasons why he would refuse to touch a weapon.

Now, in light of a possible separation from his family and village, he wanted to summarize what had transpired during the past six months, so he wrote a letter to "Simone," a false name for Robert, the brother who had so generously supported him when he had been a student and whom, of all his siblings, he had always been the closest to. André used the pseudonym "Simone" because, well, who knew what might happen to the members of his family or to the things on his desk if he were arrested?

Le Chambon, February 1943

Dear Simone,

Today I have a bit more time to write to you, and that makes me happy. I want to try to compose a little chronicle of the Trocmés in Le Chambon for you, if I'm able to actually complete it.

First, the concerns. Health: the children are doing well; actually, very well. The parents much less so. Magda is constantly stressed. She is thin, she doesn't eat well, and she is quickly aging, so that we are all seriously worried about her. A visit to the doctor in Lyon offered some comfort: there is nothing life-threatening about this rapid aging. Less work; less stress on her nerves; more rest.

I myself have been completely overworked to the point of collapse—on the Sunday before Christmas I fainted and fell off the pulpit. After that I needed to cancel all my obligations for a week. Ten days of vacation after Christmas enabled Magda and me to recover somewhat, but no sooner had we returned than my infamous back problems—which had left me in peace for three years—suddenly returned. For two weeks I had such horrible nerve pains in my stomach and bones that I could barely walk. The death of my colleague Cornier, who left behind nine children, also deeply affected me. I know that people can pull themselves out of the whirlwind, but this is impossible.

Next: Financial worries. Daily life in Le Chambon has become almost twice as expensive as it is in Paris. Naturally, we are privileged: we have potatoes, a little butter, skim milk, and some meat, in addition to the food rations. But the rations are now worthless, since things are only available at black market prices. The market opportunities provided to our farmers by the refugees and the school have fully gone to their heads. Our private family budget cannot afford those prices. Magda gives language lessons in Italian twenty-four hours every week and we have three renters, not counting the refugees, of course. We know that others are also bearing heavy burdens, but at the moment we have the feeling that we've thrown everything into a bottomless barrel—our money, our health, our future, our time together as a family, everything only for the day at hand, simply to survive.

Enough regarding material things. Turning now to our spiritual well-being: you know, perhaps, that we were able to help something like sixty Jewish refugees last summer—to hide them, provide them with food, protect them from deportation, and occasionally bring them to a safe country. You can imagine what kind of struggles with the authorities that meant for us, and the real danger we face. We have been threatened with arrest, and we have been forced to undergo long bouts of interrogation.

Of course, the fact that people can find safe haven in Le Chambon has become well known throughout all the South of France, from Nice to Toulouse and from Pau to Lyon. First dozens, then hundreds of Jews have made their way here. My normal duties as a pastor have been fully consumed. Already last summer our dining room was transformed into a waiting room, with ten or fifteen people there every day. This has now become an ongoing reality for us.

I have described for you the atmosphere of our lives, since you already know something about the larger context in which all this is taking place: 3,300 church members, including 2,000 farmers; 700 villagers; and 500 or 600 newcomers, all refugees from central Europe, including adults, youth, and children in six different houses. Add to this 300 students at the École Cévenole, along with some 30 teachers, perhaps 15 administrators of children's homes, music and choir directors, and four different scouting groups. Then there is a preparatory group of future theology students, a vocational training workshop, and soon an agricultural school. Everything is in motion, and everything passes more or less regularly through the parsonage, but we don't even know everyone's name anymore. The École Cévenole has been too successful. We could have 400 students if there weren't a shortage of accommodations. It's not only refugees we are teaching, but also children whose parents have entrusted us with their education.

In terms of group leadership, we are really quite spoiled in comparison to most other congregations. Around twenty young people who are hoping to become pastors lead, tend to, and nurture these various groups. All of the youth leaders together number about 35 people.

And what, in the midst of this whirlwind, will become of our family? We are so rarely alone with our children. We suffer from this, and they suffer from it as well. Magda and I fiercely defend our Mondays as the "pastor's Sunday," and continue to read aloud all kinds of novels to each other. But on Mondays the children are in school, and in the evenings we are so tired! Nevertheless, the children are gaining something from everything that they experience here, and they are learning the lessons of life at a very early age. Every day a whole drama plays itself out across the stage, always with new and interesting characters: a musician, a famous historian, an inventor, an artist . . .

One person is missing from André's letter: Alice Rynier, also known as Jispa. When André wrote to his brother, Jispa had been living in the parsonage for several months. But André could not have had any idea then that many of the problems he described—above all, the constant weariness and overextension—would be as good as solved the longer that Jispa lived with them.

Antoinette Butte, who later founded the religious community of Pomeyrol, met Magda at the end of 1942 and had asked her what she could do to support this completely overworked, indispensable woman. In her attempt to be helpful to Magda, Butte sent Alice Rynier, a nun, to Le Chambon. Alice had been an elementary school teacher and was preparing to serve in diaconal service during the second half of her life.

"When she suggested this to me, I was truly afraid," Magda recalled. "What should I do with a nun, who would want to spend half the day withdrawn in silent retreat? I was sure that she would not consider me to be sufficiently pious and would constantly criticize me. But then I thought a bit more and told myself that it would be idiotic to turn someone away who I desperately needed just to spare myself some criticism and an encounter with someone who was quite different from me. So I said yes."

The relationship started promptly with a mishap. On the cold January evening of Jispa's arrival, amid the completely normal chaos of the parsonage, no one remembered to pick her up at the train station. But then someone knocked at the door. A woman of about fifty years entered and greeted Magda with a smile: "Good evening, my friend!"

Magda nearly choked. "Well, she is an original!" was the thought that raced through her head.

In the first days, Magda had to swallow hard on several occasions. Alice tried to make the little ones warm up to her, but she simply did not have any spontaneous rapport with children. Indeed, the first time she took the two youngest out of the house, she lost one of them. She made up nicknames and little games—but nothing worked.

Then she created a new name for herself: Jispa, an abbreviation for "Joie de service dans la paix et l'amour" (Joy in the service of peace and love). This was not exactly the style of piety that had been nurtured in the parsonage before her arrival. But no matter. "When I'm tired, when I'm annoyed, when you are sometimes mean to me, then this name will remind me why I am here," Jispa explained.

"And this was the person who became our friend and our mother," wrote Magda years later, in the middle of the 1970s.

I had always been seeking a mother—in my teachers, in Marguerite, my father's wife . . . but in vain. However, now I found my mother, as did André, who also had been lacking a mother since he was ten years old. It is wonderful! Since then we have had the same mother—which is to say, no mother-in-law, no frustrations, no misunderstandings. In a very short time, Jispa became an essential part of our family—grandmother to all the children as well as a friend to all those in the congregation. She was supposed to stay for three months. It has now been more than thirty years.

***

Because Jispa was there, Magda was not alone with the children on the evening of February 13. It was a Saturday. André was at a meeting of those responsible for the youth work in the church. At the parsonage, someone knocked at the door. Magda opened it and found two police officers standing opposite her. "We would like to speak with your husband," one of them said.

Everyone always wanted to speak with André, so Magda was not particularly surprised. Instead, she explained that her husband would probably not return until late that evening. "But I can gladly give you whatever information you need," she offered. "I'm well informed about all the latest news."

"Thank you very much, but this has to do with something very personal," the two responded.

"Then please wait here in his workroom," said Magda, leading the men into the rear portion of the house.

She then forgot all about them.

When André returned to the house later that night, Magda was sitting at the table with her knitting. The couple spoke briefly, and it was only when André went to fetch something from the workroom that he ran into the police officers, who took him completely by surprise.

Shortly thereafter he came back to Magda. "Well, it has happened," he said. "I'm being arrested."

"Oh! And the suitcase is empty!" Magda cried.

"What kind of suitcase?" asked one of the policemen, who had walked into the kitchen.

"We've been awaiting this arrest for a long time," Magda explained, seemingly unperturbed. Already in August, soon after the visit from Lamirand and the provincial governors, Magda had packed a suitcase for André with everything that he might need in an internment camp. But since the arrest hadn't come, she had gradually taken out what André needed. And now it was completely empty.

"In the last weeks it has been so cold that I took out all the warm things from the suitcase," she now told the police officers.

"We are not in a hurry," said the other policeman. "Do everything that you think will be necessary."

Magda ran up the stairs, packed the suitcase, came back down, and looked at the coarse field peas she was preparing for supper. Even after three hours of cooking, the peas, intended as cow fodder, were still hard.

"My husband and I have not yet had a chance to eat supper," she said to the officers. "Why don't you eat with us?"

"They were amazed," she recalled later.

Policemen are probably not accustomed to being invited to a meal, especially when they have just arrested someone. I didn't do it out of generosity; it was simply time for supper. The situation was very embarrassing for the two men; one of them had tears in his eyes. Then I asked them if I could inform several of the leaders in our church. It would be difficult if my husband disappeared without any warning. "Oh, no, no! By no means! No one is allowed to know that we have arrested Monsieur Trocmé!" Only later did I discover that our house had been surrounded by police vehicles for hours.

But at precisely that moment, the doorbell rang. A young woman from the congregation, completely oblivious to the situation, stood at the threshold. She had expected Magda to open the door, but instead she stood across from two police officers. She suppressed a scream of fear, turned around swiftly, and ran back to the village. As André, Magda, and the policemen were still chewing on the tough field peas, the news spread like wildfire: they have come for the pastor!

And then the doorbell rang again. And again. One member of the congregation after another came to say goodbye to the pastor. It was a true parade. The police officers watched awkwardly from the side. They knew that their colleagues outside in the cars were also embarrassed. It was not standard procedure for an arrested person to hold court in his home before climbing into the police car. But if one was compelled to undertake this distasteful assignment, then at the least one should remain humane about it.

The guests did not stay long. Everyone embraced André briefly and placed a small gift on the table. One of the last gifts was a candle, a precious rarity in the winter of 1943. Unfortunately, there were no matches in the house.

"Then that is my contribution," said one of the police officers as he pulled a small box of matches from his pocket and set it on the table. "I will write down everything that has happened here tonight in my report."

The departure could not be postponed any longer. "May I accompany my husband for a short way?" Magda asked. Even that was granted her. "But only to the edge of the village!" they said.

As Magda, André, and the two policemen went to the door, she could hardly believe her eyes. Although it was dark, she could see that both sides of the street, for as far as she could see, were filled with people. Half the village had come running.

The four of them walked to the car between the tightly crowded rows of people. And then the Chambonnais began to sing. "C'est un rampart que notre Dieu" (A mighty fortress is our God), they sang, voices unwavering.

Magda, André, and the police officers climbed into the car.

"Well, that took a long time," said the driver as he started the engine. "Now we can finally pick up the other two." They were arresting Edouard Theis and Roger Darcissac next.

It was a few days after the arrest that André discovered the hidden value of one of the gifts he had been given that evening. It was a roll of toilet paper, a rare and valuable luxury. When he began to unroll this generous donation, he noticed there was writing on it: Bible verses.

Amid all the commotion of that night, someone in Le Chambon had scribbled verses on the thin paper, all of them on themes of hope, encouragement, and patience.

PART VI

22

Raid on the School

Saint-Paul d'Eyjeaux, 1943–Le Chambon, 1943

The excitement among the camp prisoners about the new inmates was genuine. Two pastors and a school principal had arrived! That would certainly enliven the evening discussions and keep boredom at bay.

The detainment camp in Saint-Paul d'Eyjeaux was located some three hundred kilometers (two hundred or so miles) west of Le Chambon, not far from Limoges. It was primarily intended as a prison for Communists who had been caught in a large security sweep in the winter of 1942–43. Until now there was only one Catholic priest in the camp, but even he was there as a prisoner rather than in an official capacity. Now Edouard Theis, Roger Darcissac, and André were added to the mix.

Saint-Paul d'Eyjeaux was nothing like the concentration camps in Rivesaltes or Les Milles. To be sure, the prisoners here were squeezed together in barracks, the walls and concertina wire made escape impossible, and watchtowers kept the whole camp under observation day and night. But the prisoners enjoyed certain freedoms. They were permitted visitors, and they had the right to receive mail, especially food packages. One day Magda made the long trip by train through central France, and she was somewhat comforted by what she saw. No one knew how long the detention might last, but at least the three men did not seem to be in acute danger. What they needed most was a great deal of patience. And strong nerves. Even though they had worked remarkably well together in Le Chambon during the past few months, living together in such a tiny space did not exactly provide a friendly work environment among colleagues. Magda was able to reassure the three about the state of the newly orphaned congregation. The village doctor, Dr. Le Forestier, summarized it succinctly: "The congregation of Le Chambon is not exactly the dove of the Holy Spirit. It's more like a duck: even if you cut off its head, it's still going to run for a little while."

Why were the three in this detention camp? Officially, the reason was "reeducation." But no reeducating was taking place.

Edouard Theis, Roger Darcissac, and André Trocmé in the internment camp in March 1943. Private collection.

There were no instruction sessions, no propaganda films. There were indeed some evening events, but these were organized by the prisoners themselves. There they discussed "the great revolution"—which, according to communist theory, was imminent—as well as the proper use of weapons (nonresistance played no part in the reflections of these men) and where the world was heading. The three men from Le Chambon gladly participated. Then they asked the camp administrators if they could also offer their own program. Permission was granted. So from then on they held a worship service in the camp three times a week. Roger Darcissac provided the music and singing, Edouard Theis led the liturgy, and André preached. At first only ten men participated; but then it was twenty, and then more, until finally all the wooden benches were tightly packed.

***

On March 15, a month after their arrest, the three men were surprised with good news. "You are going to be released today," a guard told them. "Your train will leave at ten o'clock in the evening."

What had happened? Who had intervened on their behalf? They had no idea. But, relieved, they packed their few belongings—blankets, tin plates, tin cups—and reported to the commander.

"Minister President Laval himself took the initiative to order your release," the commander said. "The order came from his office. Please sign your names here, and then you may go."

Roger Darcissac already had the pen in his hand when Edouard Theis suddenly became suspicious. "Sign our names?" he asked. "Exactly what are we supposed to be signing?"

"That in the future you will obey the law and will support the government under Marshal Pétain."

"But we can't sign that!" Edouard and André were in full agreement. "If we sign this and then disobey the law—which is almost inevitable—then we would be violating the ninth commandment and would be 'bearing false witness.' We do not want to be liars."

"Don't make such a fuss," said the camp commander. "Just sign and be done with it. All this is only paperwork, purely a formality."

Darcissac took the pen into his hand again and signed the form. As a teacher, he was a civil servant and obliged to obey the laws regardless. How else should he support his family if he no longer had a job as the school administrator?

Edouard and André remained firm. "Either we are released without a signature or we stay," they said.

"There's really nothing that can be done for you," muttered the commander and sent them both back to the barracks. The other prisoners could scarcely believe it.

The next morning, however, André and Edouard were called before the camp commander once again.

"Pack your things, and see to it that you leave!" the commander barked.

"Without signing anything?" the two men asked, a bit bewildered.

A low grunt from the commander was his only affirmation.

The two returned to the barracks and packed their belongings. Then they stood with the other prisoners in a circle and sang a song that they had sung so often together with the scouts in Le Chambon: "Ce ne'est qu'un au revoir" (Leave now, brothers, we don't know when you'll be back again).

Several days later, the camp was shut down. All nearly five hundred prisoners were deported to Poland.

***

On the Sunday after Edouard and André's return to Le Chambon, the church was filled to the very last seat. The newly released prisoners were properly celebrated. Yes, it seemed to be true: the congregation had moved forward courageously. But a closer look suggested a more complicated reality.

Shortly before their return, the government introduced the Service du Travail Obligatoire, an obligatory work program for young men. In Germany, factories and farms were badly in need of workers, since virtually all men capable of work were at the front. Now French young people were being recruited and sent to Germany to replace the missing farmers and factory workers—an initiative that prompted hundreds of young men to disappear "into the scrubland." The French word *maquis* refers to the impenetrable brushwood in southern France, and those who disappeared into forest—always taking a weapon for their defense—were soon known as *maquisards*.

Within weeks the word *maquis* had become a general synonym for the armed French resistance to the German occupation. André knew that many of his young church members and scouts were among the armed resistance. They had listened to him preach about nonviolence for months and seemed to have understood everything he was saying. But how should they respond now that they were being ordered to Germany to support the enemy as factory workers or farm laborers?

The church pews were indeed full, but this generation of young men was missing. Countless questions went through André's mind. What should they do now? How would they find their way through? What sort of initiatives should they be planning? England was undoubtedly informed about these matters. In any case, there were reports that the British air force was dropping weapons and supplies for the maquisards at predetermined locations. Who among the farmers in the congregation were now hiding not only Jews but also resistance fighters?

In the meantime, the first wave of refugees had already departed Le Chambon. Charles Guillon, the former mayor, was now living in Geneva—he held Swiss citizenship—and there, together with international assistants, he was organizing a systematic operation to smuggle refugees to safety. Just east of Geneva, small groups of Jewish refugees would meet a "mountain guide" who would lead them through the Savoy Alps and across the Swiss border. The attempted escapes were not always successful, and not everyone who reached Switzerland was permitted to stay. Some of them, half-starved and frozen, were sent by the Swiss authorities back across to the French side, where German soldiers awaited them.

The situation was becoming extremely complicated. It was said that Oscar Rosowsky, the chief counterfeiter of Le Chambon, had prepared more than two thousand fake documents. It was extremely doubtful that the mayor's office or the local police were ignorant of his activities. More likely, one could assume he had supporters in one or both offices—people who provided him with paper and seals, and who could, at a decisive moment, turn a blind eye to what was going on.

On the main street, in the middle of town, a curious sort of neighborhood had developed that could have led to a catastrophe at any moment. The Tante Soly inn was filled from top to bottom with Jewish children. Right next door was a house occupied by soldiers of the German Wehrmacht who had returned from the Eastern Front and were recuperating in Le Chambon.

Whenever it seemed that a raid was imminent, the Tante Soly innkeeper sent the children out the rear entrance and from there across the Lignon into the woods to "hunt for mushrooms." It is almost impossible that the soldiers never realized what was going on. They must have witnessed this parade many times. Had their experiences on the front affected the wounded soldiers so deeply that none of them was willing to betray the children?

André went dizzy when he reflected for a moment on just how many people were putting themselves into life-and-death situations. Could anyone truly bear the burden of this responsibility?

***

Things were going as they usually did—which, of course, meant anything other than a normal life. There was no time for long reflection or a careful consideration of all the options, and there was certainly not enough time for developing a grand plan or strategy. André, doing whatever was necessary for each day, simply was not capable of anything more. He knew he had to go about his work in ways that created the least possible fuss. After his internment in the prison camp, everything that happened at Le Chambon would surely be watched more closely than ever.

A new line of work had emerged. A European student aid fund had helped to transform the once-imposing Hôtel des Roches into a kind of academy. Later it came to be known as a place for an "Erasmus academic year." Students from many countries came here to live and study, each focusing on the discipline they had begun elsewhere in Europe but could no longer pursue in their homeland. Male students between the ages of twenty and thirty were housed in the thirty or more rooms. They focused on subjects like math, music, or literature. They did so without professors and with only a few books but with absolute delight that they had made it this far unscathed.

Since the spring of 1943, André's second cousin Daniel Trocmé had directed the program. The scion of an aristocratic family, Daniel was in his early thirties. He had attended an expensive residential school where he studied math and physics. Then he taught at the American school in Beirut, expanded his education with travels throughout the Near East, and served as a teacher at a French preparatory school in Rome. Daniel was considering an offer from a similar school in Barcelona as the next step in his colorful career when a letter from André reached him. An administrator was needed for the children's home in Le Chambon. Could he possibly imagine exchanging a world-famous city for a village? At least the clientele here was also international.

Daniel did not consider himself to be a Christian, at least not a Christian in the tradition of his conservative Reformed family. For him, Christendom implied a particular culture, one situated in Western civilization, which in turn was one of many civilizations with their bright and shadow sides. That had become clear to him through his travels. However, as Daniel read André's letter, he had a sudden sense of vocational calling that was so clear and compelling it surprised even himself. He agreed immediately and the same day wrote a letter to his parents.

> This morning, I threw the dice. In the first place, Le Chambon means an education for me, in the sense of participating in the reconstruction of the world. Le Chambon also means for me a very personal calling—an almost religious calling . . . actually, most definitely a religious calling. The future will show if I am up to the task—though success cannot be measured as it is in the eyes of the world. The wisdom of the world would lead me to pursue a doctorate, or at least to move to Barcelona. Le Chambon means adventure, but I have chosen this path not for the sake of the adventure, but so that I can look myself in the mirror without shame.

And so Daniel came to Les Grillons, a house in Le Chambon occupied by refugee children whose parents were interned in Gurs (if, indeed, they were still there). It was love at first sight. The children loved Daniel, and Daniel loved them. He didn't mind being on his feet around the clock, tutoring them in math during the day and then making soup for their supper in the evening. Then, while they slept, he didn't mind patching their shoes with the rubber from an old tire. Some of the children came from German Jewish families who had been driven out of Baden and the Palatinate region of Germany. The children were delighted that they could talk with Daniel in their mother tongue, since he had also attended school in Switzerland and Austria and spoke German. The other children were Spaniards, Czechs, Poles, and Austrians, and there was even a child from England.

Daniel enjoyed life in Les Grillons. "I'm not exaggerating when I say that we are truly a family here; that's the spirit that pervades everything," he wrote in a letter. "I can gladly say that I am their father—a father of twenty children who have no mother."

But then La Maison des Roches, which was what the mini university in the former hotel was now called, also needed a leader, and Daniel expressed a willingness to move back and forth between the two houses. There was simply too much work and too few people. Daniel was still young and had no family that he needed to look after. No one was aware that he suffered from a congenital heart defect; in fact, he himself had forgotten about it for weeks. "It's a ridiculous amount of work," he reported to his family, "but it's also ridiculously interesting. I like the children more and more every day, and it's extremely hard for me to acknowledge that I now have so little time for them."

Daniel was part of André's extended family, but it was Magda who had an especially warm connection with the energetic young man. The two of them got along from the first moment. She operated on a certain wavelength, and the two could instantly see things from the other's perspective.

***

Early in May 1943, a car pulled up in front of La Maison des Roches. Two German military policemen got out and asked about a German student who had fled the German Reich in opposition to National Socialism. They flashed a document and took the student away.

This is only the beginning: that thought seemed unavoidable to the students who remained. The house was no longer safe. Fortunately, it was nearly summer, so from that time forward, several of the young men slept in the woods or in a nearby farmhouse. And things stayed calm. The raid they feared did not materialize.

Until, that is, the morning of June 29. On that day, nineteen students who had dared to sleep in their own beds watched as fifteen members of the Gestapo turned the house upside down. The students were forced together into the kitchen and then interrogated, one after the other, in a small adjoining room. Daniel was not there. He had spent the night with the children at Les Grillons. People in the village sounded the alarm. "The Gestapo came to La Maison des Roches this morning at five o'clock," they told Daniel. "Don't go there! They don't know that you are the leader of the house."

"But I am the one responsible for the house," said Daniel as he set out. To his surprise, when he arrived at Les Roches, he met Magda in the kitchen. As soon as she had heard about the raid, she had jumped on her bicycle and ridden directly to the student house, her apron flapping in the wind. The Gestapo had assumed that she was the cook and had allowed her to enter the house. Now she was there as an eyewitness to what was unfolding.

From the adjoining room, one student after the other returned to the kitchen, beaten, crying, and with black eyes. One of them entrusted to Magda the address of his fiancée; another gave her his watch. Magda gathered everything in front of her on the table.

Magda was able to save one solitary student that morning. Pepito, a Spaniard, had once rescued a German soldier from drowning in the Lignon. Magda mounted her bicycle, found a witness at the hotel where the German had been stationed, and spoke so energetically to the witness that he finally agreed to go with her and to testify on Pepito's behalf. And, in fact, before they left, the Gestapo released Pepito.

Then all the students were driven to a waiting truck. Daniel went along.

"But you are not a Jew," one of the Gestapo soldiers said.

"No, but I am going to accompany my students," Daniel answered.

Then he said his goodbyes to Magda, his cousin's wife and his good friend. "Don't worry. Tell my parents that I was very happy here. It was the best time of my life. Tell them that I love to travel and that I'm on the road with friends."

23

On the Run

Le Chambon, 1943–44

The arrest of Daniel Trocmé and the students went too far. We have already lived through enough horrible things. Whom does it serve if you now add another name to the long list of martyrs?"

Maurice Rohr, a representative of church president Marc Boegner, had made a special trip to Le Chambon to safeguard André from what the church called "further stupidities." He pled now with André. "Brother Trocmé, be reasonable and go into hiding. You can't remain in Le Chambon."

"But I want to be an example," André answered. "I have preached nonresistance and now I want to hold firm to that conviction until the very end."

"And this is what you want to encourage your congregation to do as well?" Rohr asked. "A price has been put on your head. You know of course what that means: you'll be driving somewhere in the car, and then your corpse will be discovered at the edge of some forest. Or you'll be sitting at the table and your house will be stormed, which would be the end of your whole family. Are you prepared to put your wife and your children at risk just so you don't need to back off from your stubborn behavior? And above all, do you think that your congregation will hold firm to the nonviolence you've been expounding on for even one day after they discover that you've been murdered?"

"Probably not," André said hesitantly.

"Listen to me," Rohr said. "The BBC is claiming that the Allies will make a landing sometime this summer. You'll probably only need to stay hidden for a few weeks. Brother Trocmé, you are needed alive, not dead! I can promise you this: The church will pay your salary to your wife. And we will even assume all the costs of hiding you."

***

That conversation was the beginning of an odyssey. For more than ten months, André, now known as Monsieur Béguet, was on the run. It was true that the Allies were preparing for a landing at Normandy. But that didn't happen for another year, on June 6, 1944. Until the spring of 1944, André—as well as Edouard Theis, who had also been urgently counseled to leave the village—went from hiding place to hiding place.

Was it true that a price had been placed on his head? Or was that merely a claim of the maquisards, the rebel fighters, who now had free reign in the town—a ruse created with the help of their own church to get the two pastors out of the way without needing to do something to them themselves? That was also plausible. Le Chambon was no longer only the hub of nonviolent resistance, but was also a center of armed resistance. The maquisards in the area were under the leadership of Pierre Fayol, who happened to be a Jew. So the village had become a place of strategic importance.

André traveled here and there throughout the region of the Ardèche and the Drôme, constantly racked with homesickness and lower back pain. At one point during his exile, so as to keep busy, André began to develop the outlines of a far-reaching theological work. Meanwhile, Magda was on the road as a bicycle courier, and her kitchen remained central to the resistance. The parsonage continued to offer shelter and served as a crucial exchange point of information.

"The grand political events mixed themselves into the little histories of the congregation and our neighborhood," Magda wrote.

In reality, we were living multiple lives at the same time. There was the international political scene that played out between Germany and France on the battlefields, there was Pétain and de Gaulle, the BBC, and the Allies, whom we were waiting for. But there was also the parsonage with its own many small dramas: the refugees, the worries about daily bread. And then the Maquis, a second army, that derailed trains and whose members regarded themselves to be the vanguard of freedom. Many students at the École Cévenole belonged to that movement, including aspiring theologians and the school's athletic coach; even one of the scout leaders was a Maquis leader.

Early in 1944, André was not the only one suffering from homesickness. His middle son, twelve-year-old Jacques, longed so ardently for his father that Magda decided to take him to the hiding place where André was now sequestered—a castle near Die, in the Drôme region of southeastern France. Jacques was doing so poorly in school that Magda decided the only hope of improvement was if André himself tutored him.

A meeting of the parents, however, would have been too dangerous. Thus Magda accompanied Jacot, as he was known in the family, on the train only as far as Lyon, where a good friend of the family lived. The next morning André was supposed to meet Jacot at the Lyon train station, where they would continue the journey together. In the meantime, Jacot's luggage remained at the station.

Everything went as planned. André later recalled:

I arrived late, but I only needed to pick up Jacot's luggage at the baggage check. "Stay right here, I'll be right back," I said to him as I ran off. The train to Valence was supposed to leave in only a few minutes. Suddenly, I heard someone from behind shouting something, but I didn't think they were yelling at me, so I kept running. But then, without warning, I was standing face-to-face with a German soldier who was shaking with anger and pointing his gun directly at my chest. Behind me stood a second soldier, just as threatening. The first one shoved me ahead of him until I fell backward into a caged police transport. They grabbed my legs, threw me in, slammed the door, and locked it. I was trapped!

It all seemed completely absurd to me. I had been captured not because the Gestapo was looking for me but because I had run too fast. I would be interrogated and thrown into prison. My papers identified me as "Béguet," with a birthplace that I could no longer recall. I would be compelled to lie—just because of a stupidity.

But weren't the false papers, strictly speaking, also a lie? Until this moment, André had never been forced to show them. He had allowed himself to accept the falsified document only so that, if he ever had to show identity papers, the French police would not be thrown into a crisis of conscience about whether to betray the pastor trying to hide from the Germans. But now he would need to give answers and account for himself to German soldiers. No, he decided; he could not and would not go through such agony. He would simply say, "My name is not Béguet. I am Pastor Trocmé."

"Already my resolution to tell the truth soothed my conscience," he later recalled. "If God wished to do so, he could rescue me like Jonah from the belly of the whale. If not, then I did not want to defy God's will. But what about Jacot? Poor Jacot was waiting helplessly for me! At the very least, I needed to give him the baggage claim receipt so that he could claim his luggage."

Through the small barred window, André called to the soldier standing watch: "Psst. Hey, please listen to me!" How wonderful that he could speak German! "My son, a tall, blond twelve-year-old, is waiting for me at the train station," André told the soldier. "Could you please call him over here? I have to tell him what he needs to do if I'm to be arrested."

"Don't tell me any stories," the soldier replied gruffly. "Why did you run?"

"I was running to fetch a suitcase. We were trying to catch the train to Valence. Look, here is the receipt with the luggage number."

"So you weren't trying to escape the roundup?"

"What roundup?" André asked.

"Didn't you notice that the train station is surrounded by police?" the soldier asked.

"No," André responded truthfully. "I was in a hurry."

"So you're saying that you broke through the security perimeter without noticing it?" the soldier asked suspiciously. "You can't really believe that!"

"But it's the truth," André replied.

"We'll soon see about that," he said as he let André out of the van. "But don't try to run. Do that and you'll be dead."

André's account of the incident is heart-stopping.

With a rifle between my shoulder blades, I was pushed back in the direction of the train station. Hopefully, Jacot was still there!

And there he was, standing and waving to me with relief. What the soldier behind my back could not have known was that Jacot thought I had prevailed upon the man to carry our luggage. Magda had actually done that once at the train station in Valence. "That way they serve at least some kind of useful purpose," she had said when I reproached her.

"Jacot, I'm being arrested," I explained to him.

"Papa, Papa! What are we going to do?" Jacot was desperate. He screamed; he cried. And so the three of us returned together to the police van. The officer saw the child—blond, good-looking, choking with sobs.

"So it's true," he said to me. And then to the guard he said, "Bring them to the control post on the tracks. But keep an eye on them!"

The identity papers of departing travelers were being checked, but not those of arriving passengers. The departure line moved forward slowly, and André wrestled in his mind how he was going to explain to the security officer why his name was Béguet but his son was a Trocmé. As long as the soldier stood right behind him, he knew that wasn't going to work.

A column in the train station was their salvation. When the soldier began to chat with one of his colleagues, André and Jacot used the opportunity to disappear behind the pillar. From there they were able to merge unnoticed into a group of travelers who had just arrived and therefore did not need to pass through the security checkpoint. "We went down the stairs and stepped into the streetcar," André recalled. "Fifteen minutes later we were at a worship service. I took the hymnal and sang as never before in my life. It was a Sunday and I was free! Free, without needing to lie. I had escaped death! And who had saved me? It was my son, whose tears had softened the heart of an officer. It was God, who through a chain of unforeseen circumstances had made our flight possible. 'He does not want me to be dead just yet,' I said to myself."

"The time in hiding with my father was one of the best moments of my life," Jacques recalled later as an adult. "No congregation, no brothers, no sister, no mother. Just the two of us."

During this time, André wrote a short confession of faith expressing the hope that, despite everything, remained with him.

> I believe in the existence, the inherent value, and the freedom of the individual person.
>
> I believe in the existence and the inherent value of grand ideals.
>
> I believe that only one thing is truly good: that which Jesus Christ has taught.
>
> I believe that the inner life cannot be extinguished by death.
>
> I believe that in the end, good will triumph over evil.

What could André himself do to claim this victory? Not for the ultimate victory at the end of time but for the victory over the current barbarism that they all were hoping for so fervently?

Be patient. Hope. Pray.

It was not easy.

***

Approximately three kilometers (about two miles) from Le Chambon, a man was sitting at a table, writing. One of the thought leaders of the French Resistance, the man was working on a book while living in an old estate. After the war, that book would win him the Nobel Prize in Literature. At the time, however, hardly anyone in the village was aware of his presence. André and Magda were certainly not aware of him.

Albert Camus and his wife, Francine Faure, had moved from northern Algiers to Panelier, a tiny village near Le Chambon, in

August 1942 to spend the summer there. Camus suffered from tuberculosis, which had infected both of his lungs, and his doctor had urged him to escape the heat of Algeria in the summer and relocate to an area with cooler temperatures. The large house in Panelier belonged to Francine's family. From there Camus traveled every two weeks to Saint-Étienne for lung treatments. Not only was it difficult to make the trip, but the filthy industrial city depressed him anew each time he went. Nevertheless, Camus was making good progress with his writing. The central concept of the novel he had started was coming into focus, but he did not yet have a title.

At the beginning of October, Francine traveled back to Oran, Algeria. She was a teacher and needed to be at home for the start of the school year. In the interest of his health, Camus decided to stay in France another month and then join her. But early in November, British and American troops occupied Algiers, and suddenly a trip from France to Algiers became impossible. Camus was stuck in Panelier for a full year. Separated from his wife, his homeland, and all his friends, he felt trapped in a country dominated by National Socialists. This plague of Brownshirts gripped him fast, as if he were in an isolation chamber. Exactly three days after the Allied invasion of Algeria, that image led him to the central theme of his book: "The plague! They are like rats."

At a farm close to Panelier, Camus met a Jew who was hiding there. André Chouraqui was a lawyer and an extremely learned young man, preoccupied at the time with two enormous translation projects. He translated the Hebrew Scriptures into French in twenty-six volumes, and then he set about to translate the Qur'an. With Chouraqui, Camus discussed at great length the meaning of the plague in the Hebrew Scriptures that Pharaoh had stubbornly encountered as a punishment from God. Indeed, the book that Camus wrote, *La Peste*, published in 1947, would receive the English title *The Plague*.

André was completely unaware of Camus's presence nearby, but Camus fully understood the significance of the place where circumstances had forced him. And he was also aware of all the important figures from Le Chambon, many of whom appear, only slightly disguised, in his novel. In Camus's account, Paneloux (likely derived from the town of Panelier) is the name of the pastor who dares, as André had, to give an interpretation of the epidemic in a decisive sermon at the outbreak of the plague. Dr. Riou, a colleague of Dr. Le Forestier, the physician in Le Chambon, became the novel's Dr. Rieux, who personifies the character traits of Le Forestier, who had worked with Albert Schweitzer in Lambaréné, Gabon, before coming to Le Chambon. And Grand, a farmer from Panelier, lent his name to *The Plague*'s courthouse worker from Oran. Camus's Joseph Grand embodies the straightforward ethic of simple people who, without any fanfare, do the right thing. Grand stands in for all those people scattered across the plateau who willingly assumed enormous risks while shrugging their shoulders as if to say, "What was so special about that? Surely everyone would have done the same."

Camus even portrayed himself in *The Plague*. He appears as Rambert, the journalist, the only one who survives the plague, and who finds again the woman from whom he had been separated by the catastrophe.

The absurdity of the events dominates the tone of *The Plague*, which culminates with several deaths singled out amid the mass number of mortalities. At the end of the novel, Paneloux—the pastor determined to find meaning in everything that has happened, and who called his congregation to humility and penance—this same pastor is forced to witness the agonizing and painful death of a child. "Innocence has its eyes gouged out," Camus writes. Paneloux is changed.

***

In July 1944, Manou Barraud, a seventeen-year-old friend of Jean-Pierre, Magda and André's oldest son, died. Manou's mother had provided food and shelter for some young maquisards. One of them, untrained in handling weapons, as all of them were, placed his gun in a drawer with the safety off. Somehow, the gun discharged, killing the young woman.

On August 13, 1944, Jean-Pierre died in an equally absurd and tragic manner. The evening before, a Saturday, an artist had appeared in town in a theater right next to the church. In his one-man show, the artist recited and dramatized several well-known poems and fables, including the famous "Ballad of the Hanged Man" by François Villon. As he recited the poem, the artist mimed a man hanged by a rope whose body was blowing back and forth in the wind. The audience was completely rapt.

Fourteen-year-old Jean-Pierre was especially drawn to this sort of literal theater. He, the artist in the family who wrote poems and played the piano wonderfully, knew the poem by heart and recited it quietly along with the performer. On Sunday, he took a rope into the bathroom and tied it to the water tank used to flush the toilet. But as he reenacted the scene in front of the mirror, he fell off the toilet seat. When Magda found him, the cord was wrapped tightly around his neck. His feet were on the ground, but his neck had been broken.

Exactly one week later, Dr. Le Forestier died in a mass shooting at the Gestapo prison in Lyon. The exuberant, newly married man was murdered because he had provided medical assistance not only to the inhabitants of Le Chambon but also to refugees and the maquisards. At various points he'd had the opportunity to flee. But Dr. Le Forestier had made a commitment to continue helping wounded people—including wounded Germans.

The tragedies of the war continued to gather in the hearts and minds of the Chambonnais, and Magda and André grieved deeply the loss of their son.

***

A week after Dr. Le Forestier's death, military transport vehicles rolled into Le Chambon. The soldiers threw small presents from the windows as the children ran alongside the vehicles and gathered up the coffee packets, candies, chocolates, and small jars of jam.

"We're free! We're free!" The joy of the Chambonnais was boundless.

Free? André was also elated. From this day forward he could once again work as a pastor without interference. Yet he had long recognized freedom as more than an external state of being. "But we were, of course, always free!"

24

The Great River of History

From San Francisco to Hanoi, 1945–96

In 1958, André and Magda's children were adults and scattered throughout Europe and the United States. Whatever Magda and André had hoped to give to them was already given. But André still had a deep desire to summarize a few things as he saw them now, with greater distance. He took the occasion of his birthday to write several pages of reflections to them.

Versailles, April 7, 1958

Dear Nelly, dear Jacot, dear Daniel,

As of this morning at one o'clock I am now 57 years old. That is, of course, not a particularly remarkable age, but since Maman and I are together on my birthday for the first time in many years and are celebrating together, I am writing a somewhat celebrative letter. . . . I don't have any illusions: My birth was a tiny event in the great river of history that carries along generations of people across thousands of years. I often have to pinch myself to confirm that I really do exist and that what I experience right now is real and true. It has become my habit to reflect ceaselessly on life, death, people, and things—trying to find common themes, trying to fathom their meaning . . . This is my greatest pleasure and a constant temptation. Fortunately, I married a woman who lives completely in the moment, a person for whom life, and people, and things are always fully in the moment and who pulls me out of my rather sterile and egotistical reflections.

In these reflections, André wrote of the "game of life: marriage, raising children, forgetting about oneself," and noted that he had always dreamed of a retreat, which never materialized for him. Even now, thirteen years after the end of the war, he described himself as if he were still living amid the whirlwind—and he addressed his children as if the same were true for them. "There is not much time remaining for me to do those things for which I was put here to do," he wrote. "I have not done anything very great. Perhaps I did contribute a little bit to help overcome the narrowmindedness of a certain form of French Protestantism."

More than anything else, however, the letter was a hymn of praise to Magda and to the "stroke of good luck" that the marriage had meant for André's life.

I also need to pinch myself when I think about the events surrounding our marriage. The risks seemed enormous to me. I was not sure at all about things, even though I was completely in love. In the middle of that strange year in New York we became engaged. In those days I often dreamed with my eyes wide open. But Maman had her feet planted firmly on the ground, and the first gift that she provided me was to call out to me: "Hey! I'm here! I actually do exist! Wake up!" It took me several years to wake up, and that was sometimes unpleasant, since the presence of another person is disruptive. Another's claims and character (which we always find to be worse than our own) interfere with the wonderful monologue that we would so love to carry on for ourselves alone.

In my mid-thirties, I fought to bring my "Christian dream," which I didn't want to relinquish, into alignment with the realities of life, especially the presence of four flesh-and-blood human beings: Nelly, Jean-Pierre, Jacot, and Daniel. However, in so doing I made a great discovery: every other person existed just as I did, was just as unique and important as me. Now I knew what love meant: to regard another person as you regard yourself; to actually put yourself into their situation instead of just dreaming that you love them. To serve them. And so I came to recognize that Maman, in the midst of all the challenges that she faced, was always the more loving one in actual practice—and therefore the more Christian. . . .

Even though it sounds strange, it was the war that brought us what we were lacking: in an effort to save lives, we finally were

André Trocmé in his office in Geneva. Private collection.

able to reconcile dream and reality. The truth of God—that is, the other: the other human, the Jew, whom one hides. In so doing, you accept a certain risk for yourself in the process. All that exists had become more precious to me.

But then Jean-Pierre died, and I was like a tree destroyed by a lightning bolt, while Maman, in order not to cry, worked herself nearly to death. I could not comfort myself, as others have done, by saying his life was also complete. My little Jean-Pierre did not live a full life.

André whitewashed nothing. Nor did he write with a tone of resignation. Things in political and church life after the war were not suddenly in order. Indeed, the acts of revenge by the maquisards on those who refused to support them or who had betrayed their cause were not much less brutal than the horrors those on the plateau had endured during the war. As soon as the occupiers left, those who remained behind settled their grievances without mercy.

André tried to intercede, to soften the tone, to bring people together in conversation. He also worked for reconciliation in yet another area. Toward the end of the war, he had started to hold worship services with German prisoners of war who were being held in a prison camp not far from Le Chambon. André preached in German, something that made people in his own congregation suspicious. How was one to know exactly what André was telling the prisoners? After all, he himself was half *Boche*, as the Germans were derisively known.

The 120 prisoners of war being held near Le Chambon had been charged with the most horrible crimes. They were now being guarded by the same French police offers who, only a few months earlier, had obeyed German orders (at least indirectly, under the Vichy regime). In a similar context, in the region of Ardèche, policemen took revenge on German prisoners by lynching them.

The atmosphere in Le Chambon was also extremely tense. So André tried to defuse tensions by bringing people together. Ms. Höfert, the German teacher at the École Cévenole, created two written versions of André's sermons—one in French and one in German. That way, every Sunday morning André gave the same sermon in French to the congregation at Le Chambon that he gave in the afternoon in German at the prison. The presence of bilingual witnesses helped to lessen the suspicions that he was telling the German prisoners something different from what he was telling his congregation.

In the aftermath of the war, André also decided to do a series of sermons on the Ten Commandments and, in the process, he developed a kind of basic course in Christian faith—which, nonetheless, met with rejection on both sides. In the church in Le Chambon, there were many maquisards, who relinquished their weapons in the foyer only under duress since André did not allow them to sit armed in the church pews. "The gospel is wonderful in theory," the rebel fighters would say. "But in practice . . . think for a moment of all the massacres; think about the gas chambers! Tell all this to the Germans!" Such comments invariably followed his Sunday morning service.

Then in the afternoon, at the camp for German prisoners of war, the refrain went: "You don't need to be preaching this to us! Tell it instead to your dear friends, the Communists. Some day you are going to be thankful that we protected you from the Communists."

And so, in 1945, André found himself once again occupying a place familiar to him since before the war: a space between all parties. And there he stayed, no matter where he found himself in the coming decades. He and Magda would move away from Le Chambon in their later years, but their experience of standing between opposing factions remained with them. Regardless of how many successes André celebrated—how many cities he visited throughout the world, how many people in Tokyo, Stockholm, Algiers, or Tel Aviv listened to his lectures, or how many honors he received—no matter these things, the Reformed Church of France remained uneasy about him.

***

After André and Magda had worked for several years for the International Fellowship of Reconciliation in Versailles, André accepted a pastorate in Geneva, Switzerland, and Magda began to once again teach Italian in a preparatory school. From 1960 until his retirement in 1970, André served as the pastor in Saint-Gervais, a congregation near the Geneva central train station, even as he continued to travel tirelessly. The themes of peace and nonresistance remained at the center of his work. Sometimes he traveled with Magda; sometimes they traveled independently.

And what became of the dream that they would visit India together to meet personally with Mahatma Gandhi? Magda and André had not forgotten about it, and it almost came to pass. Throughout the years, they frequently talked about their derailed honeymoon plans of 1926. However, other concerns demanded their attention now as well. The École Cévenole was struggling financially, and considering the grim circumstances in Europe, it was almost impossible to raise money locally. So toward the end of 1945, André traveled to the United States to seek support for the school. In fact, a circle of supporters did emerge that ensured the long-term survival of the school.

André's biggest wish, however, was to see Germany again. The land of his mother and the land where the war had begun was a place he had yearned for since childhood. It was not until his second trip there after the war, in 1949, that he could see that tongues were slowly loosening and that Germans were beginning to ask self-critical questions about their role in the atrocities: What did we know? What could we have known? Why was there so little protest? Why was the Confessing Church so small?

"The first priority is to teach children that conformity and fear are the sins that weigh heaviest," André wrote, reflecting on the trip. "An interpretation of the Ten Commandments that reduces sin only to those things that are detrimental to the individual or personal well-being is completely misguided. Refusal to conform for reasons of conscience is the first obligation of anyone who is a follower of Jesus. The second most serious sin is complicity with injustice—exploiting or degrading another person, standing silent in the face of wrong—those are the things for which our society must be ashamed."

Only then did India come once again into view, even though Gandhi had been assassinated. In 1949, Magda traveled to India as the French representative to a global peace forum. There she met with some of Gandhi's students not long after the death of their teacher. It was an unforgettable experience that prompted Magda to spend nearly half a year in India and the newly established state of Pakistan. Meanwhile, André traveled elsewhere in the world, including Japan and Indochina (today Laos, Cambodia, and Vietnam). In many detailed letters to each other, they described their observations and travel experiences.

André's thoughts returned repeatedly to developments in Germany. "The idealism of German youth is not dead," he wrote. "They are fully prepared to become enthralled with other big ideas. But the Protestant church offers them nothing other than a very theological, very abstract faith. If we could send a dozen young, engaged Christians with thoughtful pacifist convictions to Germany, they would reap a very rich harvest."

Magda Trocmé (second from left) meeting with the last governor-general of India, Chakravarti Rajagopalachari (center), and Indira Gandhi (right), who later became prime minister. Private collection.

In a letter to André written in India in 1949, Magda reflected, "Godse, Gandhi's murderer, was hanged along with his accomplice on November 15. What would have Gandhi said about that?"

Magda's and André's travels around the world continued. Four years later, Magda wrote to André from Pennsylvania: "Along with my guide I visited two Amish farmsteads and felt as if I had suddenly been transported into a Darbyist household in the plateau. The same strict simplicity, the same rough-hewn table without a tablecloth, the same cleanliness."

André also traveled to the United States. "I have the feeling that the word *war* is an abstraction here, something that people have simply grown accustomed to," he wrote. "In Europe it is a terrifying word, one that denotes a scourge of humanity, and in the face of which one despairs."

André searched everywhere for allies, and he found them. In 1957, along with German Mennonites, he helped to found an organization Eirene, which helped conscientious objectors to war in Morocco have the option of civilian service. Along the way came new themes and new tasks, which Magda and André engaged without losing sight of the old. In the 1960s, the emancipation of African Americans rose to the center of their attention, and Magda spoke at massive gatherings alongside Martin Luther King Jr. in the United States. This was followed by their involvement in the early years of the anti–nuclear power movement.

In the meantime, both Magda and André had retired. For the first time in their adult lives, they could do what they wanted, whatever seemed most important to them. But didn't they feel tired? Wasn't it time to truly rest?

André Trocmé with a young boy in Hiroshima, Japan. Private collection.

"With age one needs to become more tolerant," André wrote in a letter to Nelly on the occasion of her fortieth birthday.

Otherwise, you cut yourself off from the rest of humanity and become bitter. You have to learn to laugh at yourself, especially at the mistakes that you have come to know so well, or at your own narrow perspective, at the limitations that ultimately mean you can no longer become anyone other than the person you have already become. And above all things, you must live for others, of your own free will, of course, since those who instinctively hold on to the egoism of their youth in their older years have no future at all. To know your limits and not forget that you need to constantly seek out new sources of "fuel" by listening to others and finding in their words, their courage, and their beliefs examples that you can follow.

By then Magda and André had already become exemplars, providing fuel to others. In January 1971, André was supposed to travel to Yad Vashem, the Holocaust memorial center in Israel, to receive a Righteous Among the Nations medal. This honor was given to non-Jews who, at great risk to themselves, assisted Jews during the Holocaust. But André resisted the invitation. If someone wished to honor what had happened in Le Chambon, he reasoned, then the celebration should take place in Le Chambon and the medal be given to the whole town—indeed, to the whole plateau.

Eventually, André and Yad Vashem agreed on a date in May for him to travel to Israel to receive the medal, but by then André was too sick to travel. His old problems with back pain had restricted him so much that he finally agreed to an operation at a hospital in Geneva. Through a medical error, the operation was a failure; two additional operations followed, but André remained a paraplegic. He spent five weeks either in bed or in a wheelchair.

Nevertheless, he preached for his fellow patients at the hospital worship services, and he began writing the book whose basic outline he had developed while in prison during the war.

André died suddenly on June 5, 1971, of a blood clot in his lung. "I had a good life," he said to Nelly in their last conversation together. "But before I die, I would like to know very much how the Israelis and the Palestinians are going to resolve their problems."

A week later, as he was carried to his grave in Le Chambon, Magda received the medal of the Righteous Among the Nations on his behalf.

***

After André's death, Magda and Jispa moved to Paris. From there Magda continued to pursue a host of activities. Still, every summer she would take a break and travel with Jispa to Le Chambon

Magda Trocmé after accepting an honorary doctorate at Haverford College, 1981. Private collection.

for an entire month. There Magda would take a rocking chair on Sunday mornings and sit outside the church door after the worship service, greeting everyone who left the church. During the midweek market, she would do the same thing, sitting on her chair in the marketplace and greeting everyone who passed by.

Magda traveled to the United States on three more occasions. In 1981, she flew to Pennsylvania to accept an honorary doctorate from Haverford College—in the name of all the inhabitants of Le Chambon and the neighboring villages. Another elderly woman was honored alongside her: Rosa Parks, who had refused to yield her seat on a bus to a white passenger in 1955 and had become a guiding star in the constellation of the civil rights movement.

In 1984, Magda also received the medal of the Righteous Among the Nations, which she accepted not in Israel but in the Israeli consulate in Paris. "Not for me," she emphasized, "but as a representative of the entire plateau." That same year she traveled to Washington, D.C., to participate in a peace conference along

Magda Trocmé in 1974.
Private collection.

with Jewish writer Elie Wiesel, who would receive the Nobel Peace Prize two years later. In 1986, Magda's third trip to the United States was to visit Nelly and her American grandchildren.

In her final years, Magda lived with her son Jacot near Paris, where she died on October 10, 1996, shortly before her ninety-fifth birthday. In the summer of 1997, her ashes were interred in the family grave in Le Chambon. In a joyful celebration, her children, ten grandchildren, many great-grandchildren, and relatives from Italy, Sweden, Germany, and the United States, along with many inhabitants of Le Chambon, took their leave of a woman who had become a legend.

***

Long before her death, Magda had summarized in two sentences the values and beliefs she regarded as important—what she wanted to pass along to future generations. She had written these on cards for each child and grandchild. Now, after her death, the cards were passed out to her children and grandchildren. Each card carried the same text: "The ideals, the hopes, the yearning for justice, truth, and love that we all sense, regardless of religion or culture, would not be rooted so deeply within us if there wasn't also somewhere a source of this hope, of justice, of truth, and of love. This source is what I call God."

It was that source in which she had found the strength and motivation for her entire life.

Whenever people asked André about his or Magda's role in the resistance movement or in the global pacifist movement, or expressed amazement at the energy that seemed to drive them both, André always told a little story about a monk and a bird.

A Buddhist monk sat at the edge of the Yellow River and watched a dove with amazement. At regular intervals, the bird dipped its plumage into the water and then flew up into the air, feathers sparkling with water. And then he returned to do it again.

"Why are you doing that?" the monk asked the dove.

"Don't you see the smoke on the horizon?" the bird answered. "There's a forest fire over there. I'm trying to put it out."

The monk laughed out loud. "And you, little bird, think that you can do something about it?"

"I don't know," said the dove. "But I know that I have to try."

Epilogue

What happened to the various people and organizations that André and Magda's lives touched?

Nelly, the Trocmés' daughter, traveled as an au pair to the United States, where she studied and later married. She worked for many years as a French teacher. Nelly is the mother of three children and lives today in Saint Paul, Minnesota.

Daniel went to study in the United States, married a Swedish woman, and became the father of two children. He died in Denver, Colorado, in 1962.

Jacques (known as Jacot) also studied in the United States. He married an American and they moved to Europe near Paris. Today he lives in southern France.

Jispa stayed with Magda long after André's death, living alongside her closest friend for forty-three years. Jispa died in 1989 at the age of ninety-six and was interred in the Trocmé family grave.

Edouard Theis continued as the dean of the École Cévenole until his retirement in 1964. His wife, Mildred, died in 1973; he died in 1984. To protect their daughters from the war, a family friend took six of the daughters to the United States, the homeland of their mother, in 1940. Only the second youngest, who was then three years old, and the youngest child, who was born a month after her older sisters departed, remained in France until the end of the war. In 1945, four of the daughters returned from the United States to France. The two oldest had already started their studies in the United States, where they married and are still living today. The others remained in France. One of the daughters is now deceased.

After the war, it was revealed that **Marc Boegner** had been the one who had arranged for the release of André, Edouard Theis, and Roger Darcissac from the prison in Saint-Paul d'Eyjeaux by drawing on his good connections with the Vichy government. He remained the leader of the Reformed Church of France until 1961. For many years Boegner was also in the international council of the Reformed Church and active as a guest professor on the international law faculty at The Hague. During the second Vatican Council, he served as an official Protestant observer. He died in 1970. For his efforts on behalf of the Jews, Boegner was honored by Yad Vashem in 1988 as one of the Righteous Among the Nations.

After his efforts to support Jewish refugees in Valence through the activities of the YMCA and CIMADE, **Charles Guillon** moved to Geneva, where he was active in the International Red Cross. After helping many people escape France, he was forced to go underground. After the war, the highly esteemed "Uncle Charles" again became the mayor of Le Chambon and remained in that position until his death in 1959. In 1991, Yad Vashem honored him as one of the Righteous Among the Nations.

All eighteen students (four French and fourteen foreigners) who were taken during the raid on **La Maison des Roches** were sent to concentration camps. Of these, four went to Auschwitz. Any trace of six others was lost. Eight survived and were freed at the end of the war. **Daniel Trocmé** was sent first to a French prison and then to Buchenwald, and later to the Majdanek concentration camp, on the outskirts of the city of Lublin, Poland. He died there on May 2, 1944. Yad Vashem awarded Daniel the posthumous honor of the Righteous Among the Nations in 1976.

The soldier who lost sight of André and Jacot in Lyon and made possible their escape was transferred to the Eastern Front. While the three were waiting at the security checkpoint, the officer who had remained in the car reviewed photos from the wanted list and recognized André. By the time he arrived at the tracks, however, all traces of André and Jacot were gone. A historian who studied the history of the resistance discovered the incident in the archives of the Gestapo in Lyon and told André about it later.

The École Nouvelle Cévenole operated until July 2014. During the school year, students from thirty nations studied there. In the summer the school hosted camps and conferences oriented around the themes of peace and nonresistance. After the murder of one student by another in November 2011, the school was forced to close its doors.

Eirene, the organization that André founded with the help of German Mennonites, continues to be an international, ecumenical peace and development program that sends young people from Germany throughout the world to do peace-related service work. See www.eirene.org.

The International Fellowship of Reconciliation also still exists. The organization understands itself to be "an association of people who, on the basis of their religious convictions or humanitarian beliefs, are committed to a nonviolent way of life and to nonviolence as a means of personal, social, and political change." In the summer of 2014, IFOR celebrated its one hundredth anniversary.

In the summer of 2013, the **Lieu de Mémoire**, a museum and place of memory, was established in Le Chambon. Anyone traveling to Le Chambon will find it much easier to follow the traces left behind by Magda, André, and many others. See www .memoireduchambon.com.

Acknowledgments
and Sources

Oral sources

The number of eyewitnesses still alive after seventy years is naturally quite small. Thus I am all the more grateful to all those in Le Chambon whom I learned to know personally in the summer of 2010 and who were willing to talk about their childhood and youth during those years. Rolande Lombard, a doctor and friend of Magda Trocmé who was several years younger than Magda, was willing to share with me her memories of the Trocmé and Theis families, as well as details related to the school. Ariane Tuffrau, a godchild of André Trocmé, made available her photographs from the 1940s. Like Madame Tuffrau, René Rivère is still living today in the same farmstead where people were hidden throughout the war. As a school friend of the Trocmé children, he told me many stories and helped to paint a vivid picture of life in a Huguenot family.

I also want to thank Gérard Bollon, a local historian and the most knowledgeable person regarding the history of Le Chambon and the resistance, for the time and attention that he gave to this project. Likewise, thanks to Amélie Baudraz-Bruderer, who accompanied me on my search for evidence throughout the Massif Central Mountains.

Written sources

My two most important written sources were the recollections of Magda and André Trocmé, resources from which I drew most of the dialogue that appears in the book, using their words as exactly as possible and noting them with quotation marks. The "Souvenirs" (Magda) and "Mémoires" (André) have never been published and were originally intended only for a small circle of friends and family. Both of these unfinished volumes were donated by Magda to the Peace Collection of the library at Swarthmore College, near Philadelphia. The library continues to focus its holdings on pacifist authors (see www.swarthmore.edu/library/peace). Copies of both books can also be found in the archives of the library of the World Council of Churches in Geneva, where I had access to them.

The second most important source for me was the book by Pierre Boismorand, *Magda et André Trocmé: Figures de résistance* (2007). The book is a gathering of texts with commentary compiled by Boismorand, a Swiss pastor.

Das Dorf auf dem Berge by Johan Maarten (that is, Otto Bruder, aka Otto Salomon) can be found in rare book shops. The last German edition was published by Brendow Verlag (1984).

Six months after the first edition of this book was published, Stefanie Huesmann published an academic work about Peter Brunner, a Hessian pastor who later became a professor of theology. Huesmann's book, drawing extensively on written sources and contemporary interviews, provides a close reading of *Das Dorf auf dem Berge*. Her book is *Mut zum Bekenntnis: Peter Brunner's Widerstand im aufkommenden Nationalsozialismus* (2012).

At the end of the 1970s, American author Philip Hallie made his way to Le Chambon to conduct research. Hallie had fought with the U.S. Army during World War II. After the war, as a professor of philosophy, he focused his studies especially on cruelty and ethical behavior. *Lest Innocent Blood Be Shed* (1979) is the only book on the history of the plateau that has also appeared in German.

Some thirty years after Hallie, another professor from the United States made the trip to Le Chambon. In *We Only Know Men: The Rescue of Jews in France during the Holocaust* (2007), Patrick Henry presents several impressive biographical sketches of prominent, albeit little-known, figures of nonviolent resistance—including Magda, André, and Daniel Trocmé—within the context of the most recent historical research. I am indebted to Henry's book for the information about Albert Camus's years in the plateau.

Of enormous help to me was a book available to me only in digital format because it did not appear in print in the United States until April 2012. Richard Unsworth brings together detailed and precise research in a far-ranging analysis called *A Portrait of Pacifists: Le Chambon, the Holocaust, and the Lives of André and Magda Trocmé*. Unsworth's work places Magda as an equal partner alongside André.

Yet another very readable and richly illustrated book, even though it was published by a small press as local history, is the volume by Annick Flaud and Gérard Bollon, *Paroles de réfugiés, paroles de justes: La montagne dans la guerre, terre d'exil, terre d'asile autour du Chambon-sur-Lignon* (2009). The book offers portraits of those who survived because they were able to hide in the plateau.

Alicia J. Batten, professor of religious studies at the University of Sudbury in Ontario, Canada, published a compact, richly footnoted study of only twenty pages that is nonetheless good to read: "Reading the Bible in Occupied France: André Trocmé and Le Chambon," *Harvard Theological Review* 103, no. 3 (2010): 309–28. I found a short, insightful survey of French history during the Vichy period in Henry Rousso's *Vichy: Frankreich unter deutscher Besatzung, 1940–1944* (2009).

There are also books for youth and children that recount what happened on the plateau, including *Hidden on the Mountain* (2007) by Deborah Durland DeSaix and Karen Gray Ruelle and *Greater Than Angels* (1999) by Carol Matas.

One of the children who was hidden and who later moved to the United States took the initiative to ensure that a room in the Holocaust Memorial Museum in Washington, D.C., was dedicated to Le Chambon. More information about this can be found at www.ushmm.org. The webpage that Yad Vashem has dedicated to the events in and around Le Chambon can be found at www .yadvashem.org/righteous.

André Trocmé wrote frequently, and he enjoyed writing. Nevertheless, only two books by him appeared during his lifetime: *La politique de la repentance* (1953) and *Jésus-Christ et la revolution non violente* (1961). The latter presents the foundations of Christian pacifism in a systematic fashion and is available in English as *Jesus and the Nonviolent Revolution*.

Films

The documentary film *Weapons of the Spirit* by Pierre Sauvage is definitely worth seeing. Sauvage was born near the end of the war to a Jewish couple hiding in Le Chambon. They were able to immigrate to the United States after the occupation. In the 1980s, Sauvage traveled back to the place of his birth to search for evidence about that time and to meet the people who had saved his life.

The fate of the children who were hidden in Le Chambon is told in *The Hill of a Thousand Children* (French with English subtitles).

Stories by André Trocmé

During the Christmas season, André often told the children of Le Chambon stories that he made up. After the war he wrote these down and added several new stories to the collection. Even though these stories were originally envisioned for children, André's ability to weave biblical material into themes that mattered to the people of his congregation meant that the stories also attracted the attention of adults. These tales, preserved by his daughter, were published in English as *Angels and Donkeys: Tales for Christmas and Other Times* (2002).

The Author

Hanna Schott is a journalist, writer, and editor living in Haan, Germany. She studied French, Italian, music, and theology at universities in Marburg, Freiburg, and Heidelberg. Schott has worked as a bookseller and is the author of many books. She is a member of Evangelische Kirchengemeinde St. Reinoldi Rupelrath.

Find discussion questions for this book at HeraldPress.com/ StudyGuides.